CHAPTER BY CHAPTER

We are always adding to our life story.

SCHOLASTIC
LITERACY PLACE®

Copyright © 1996 by Scholastic Inc.   All rights reserved.   Printed in the U.S.A.
                                             ISBN 0-590-48656-X
                  6 7 8 9 10   24   02 01 00

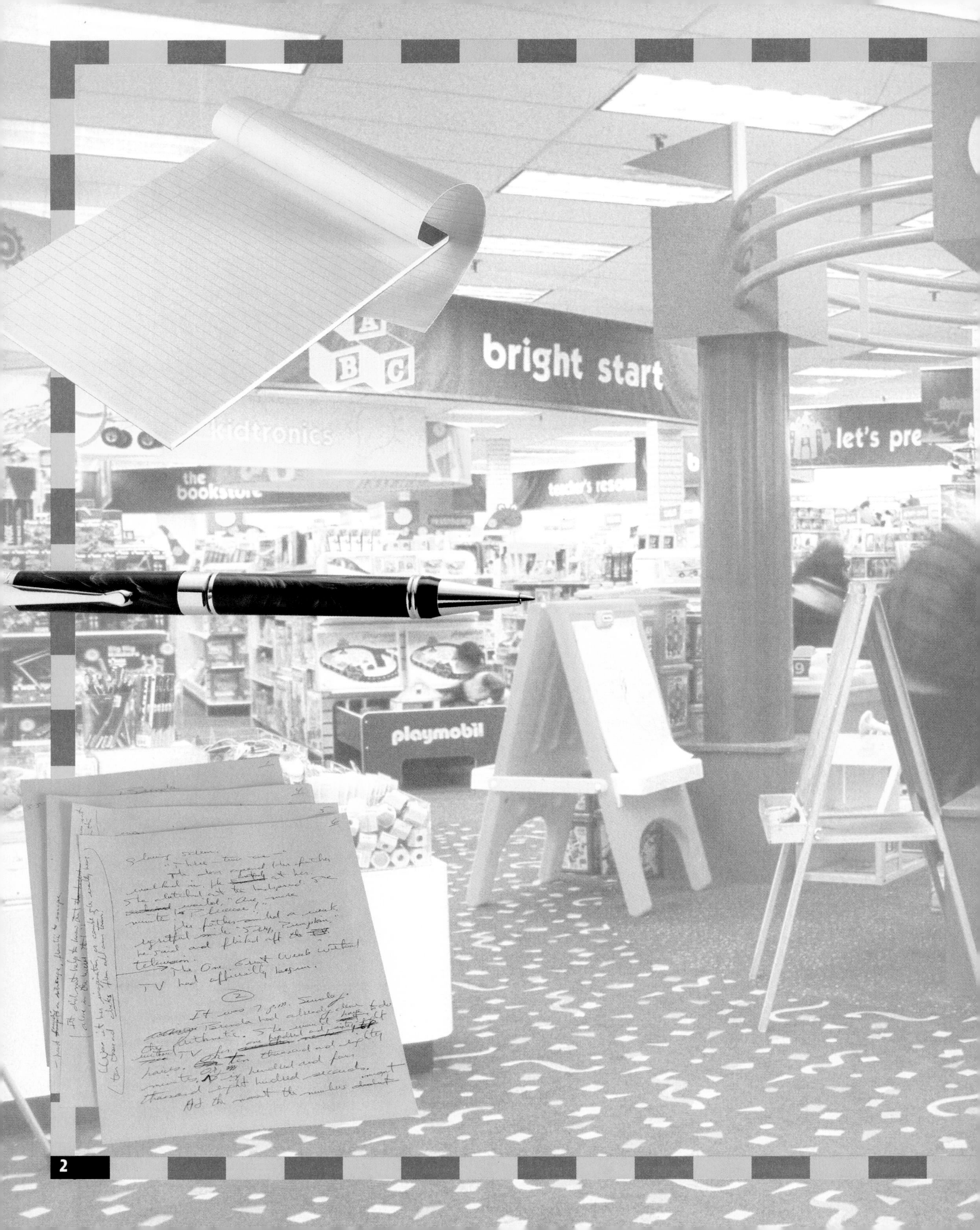
bright start
kidtronics
the bookstore
playmobil

Browse
in a Bookstore

We are always adding to our life story.

Ready, Set, Grow

We have many thoughts about growing up.

SOURCE Novel

Class-Picture-Taking Day

10

by Pam Conrad
illustrated by Joel Spector

from *Staying Nine*

SOURCE Reference Book

The Inside Story: Science Facts About Growing Up

22

from *Big Science*

SOURCE Personal Anecdotes

Tales of a Fourth Grade Rat

24

told by Jerry Spinelli

MENTOR Author

Jerry Spinelli

30

WORKSHOP 1

How to Create a Table of Contents

34

With a Little Help

We can look to older people for help.

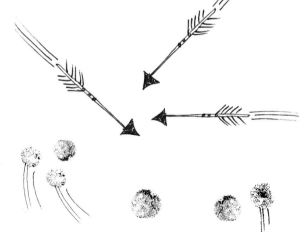

When I Was Nine
by James Stevenson

A Pocketful of Memories

Families and traditions are an important part of who we are.

Trade Books

The following books accompany this *Chapter by Chapter* SourceBook.

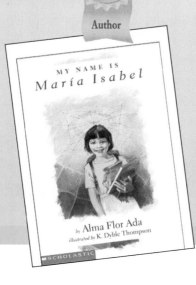

Before The Nine O'Clock Bell
Wooster Scott

We have many thoughts about growing up.

Ready, Set, Grow

Meet a girl who wants to stay nine forever. Then learn how fast your bones can grow.

Find out what fourth grade was like for author Jerry Spinelli.

Visit Jerry Spinelli at home and meet his pet chinchilla, Chi-Chi.

WORKSHOP 1

Create a Table of Contents for your life story.

Contents

from STAYING NINE

CLASS-PICTURE-TAKING DAY

By
Pam Conrad

Illustrated by
Joel Spector

AWARD WINNING

Author

Heather likes being nine. She's worried about turning ten in another week—so worried that she wants time to stand still. Today is class-picture-taking day, and Heather has decided to wear the same clothes that she wore for last year's picture. The only problem is that she and her friend Dorelle had planned to wear identical outfits.

H eather put the chewable vitamin right on the side of her mouth, over the tooth that was loose, and she bit hard, making it pinch.

"But I thought you and Dorelle were going to wear the same outfits," her mother was saying. "Didn't you say you wanted to look like twins? Same clothes? Same hairdo?"

Heather took a mouthful of scrambled eggs. "I changed my mind," she said.

"But Heather, those clothes have been in your closet for months. I can't remember the last time you wore them. And they look all wrinkled, like you slept in them!"

"These clothes fit me just fine. I haven't worn them in a while, but I haven't grown at all since the last time. It's what I want to wear." Heather kept eating, hoping her mother wouldn't force her to change and ruin everything.

"What about Dorelle?" her mother asked, taking a different view. "Isn't she expecting you to wear—"

"Ma!" Sam looked up suddenly from her homework notes that were spread out across the breakfast table, scattering cereal onto the floor. "You have to let her wear what she feels good in," she said. "This is a sign of growing interference."

"I think you mean growing *independence*," Mrs. Fitz said, pouring herself a cup of coffee and tapping meaningfully on the dictionary that was propped up in front of Sam. Then she turned back to Heather with a puzzled expression. "Well, I guess it *is* up to you, dear. It's just I think it's silly to wear old clothes to have your picture taken, especially when you already promised somebody—"

"No, Ma, it's growing *interference*," Sam said, pointing to a page in the dictionary. "It says here, 'Interference: taking part in other people's affairs without invitation.'"

Heather smiled a little and kept her head down.

"Well, excuse me!" their mother said, narrowing her eyes at Sam. "If I get in the way around here, you'll let me know, won't you?"

"No problem," Sam answered as she got up, stacking her books and taking a last drink of her juice. "You will be *notarized* if you get in the way."

"Notified," Mrs. Fitz corrected, clearing off the table brusquely. "Now both of you get out of here, or you'll be late for the halls of academia."

"Halls of academia?" Sam stared at her mother.

"Look it up," Mrs. Fitz said in a clipped voice. "Not now!" she fussed, when Sam sat down again. Mrs. Fitz put the dictionary back in the pile and eased Sam toward the door. "Come on, Heather," she added. "It's time to pack up and leave. You don't want to be late for the photographer."

It was a cold, gray day, and Heather walked along quickly with her backpack over her shoulders and her hands thrust into her pockets.

She was feeling pretty good, satisfied with herself and content. In a word, she was feeling nine. She was holding on to nine without any problem at all. No problem, that is, until she got to the school yard and saw Dorelle waiting for her at the front gate.

"I thought you'd *never* get here," Dorelle called, waving her hand, and then her wave stopped in midair. Her smile vanished. "Your hair! You said you'd wear it loose today. You said you'd just let it be curly."

Heather smoothed her hand along the side of her head, pushing any stray strands back toward her ponytail. She felt a little uneasy. "I changed my mind, and it was late by the time I decided, so I couldn't call you."

"What do you mean you changed your mind?" Dorelle's face looked angry and tight. Her hair wasn't naturally curly like Heather's, and Heather could tell Dorelle's mother had probably set it the night before. It curled all over the place, framing her squinting eyes and her furious mouth.

Heather looked off into the distance, staring at the kids who were chasing each other across the school yard. She shrugged. She didn't know what to say. She didn't know how to explain it. After all, Dorelle had turned ten a few months ago. She'd had a skating party, and Dorelle had even whispered to Heather that she almost felt like a teenager now that she had two digits in her age. How do you explain staying nine and not changing to someone like that? Heather shrugged and looked back at her friend. "I don't know. I just changed my mind. I decided to wear the same thing I wore for last year's picture."

Dorelle's mouth fell open. "The same thing? You're wearing the same thing, the exact same thing as *last* year?"

Heather nodded. It still didn't sound at all stupid to her. What was the big deal?

Dorelle's face grew small and mean. "I should have been twins with Lauren," she said slowly. "I never should have been twins with you!" And at that Dorelle turned and walked away from Heather. Heather could see her dark skirt, and her white tights, the gray shoes, and the little pink barrette in her hair.

I guess I should have called, she thought with an awful sinking feeling inside; and letting the backpack slide down her arms, she grabbed the straps with her hands. The school bell rang and she headed for her classroom.

Mrs. Kleintoch was waiting at the door, and Heather had to look at her twice. Was it really Mrs. Kleintoch? She had blue eye shadow on her lids and a sparkly earring showing through her hair beneath each ear. She patted Heather's shoulder as she passed, and Heather noticed the red nail polish and the unfamiliar perfume.

"Let's hurry, people," she was saying. "We have a lot to do today, and we're the first class to be photographed, so we need to get our things in order and line up right away."

Everyone was beginning to line up, and Heather looked around. Dorelle was whispering to Lauren over by the pencil sharpener. Heather looked away. And then she saw Sonya. Sonya's desk was right next to Heather's, and she usually wore her hair kind of plain, but today she had about three hundred little braids all over her head, and at the end of each braid was a tiny bead.

"Oh, your hair is beautiful!" Heather said, delicately touching the beads with her fingers and seeing them clink against each other.

Sonya smiled broadly. "My mother said I could wear my hair like this when I was ten years old, for my ten-year-old picture. She would never do it before. Said it was too much trouble to do on someone so little, but now I'm old enough."

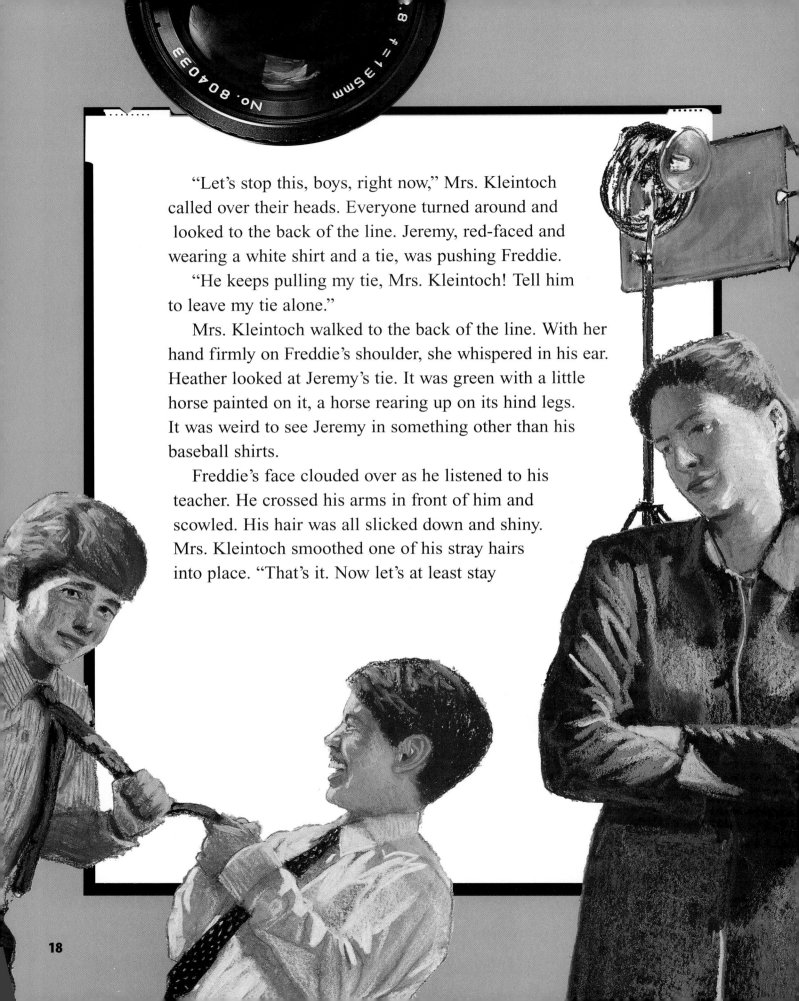

"Let's stop this, boys, right now," Mrs. Kleintoch called over their heads. Everyone turned around and looked to the back of the line. Jeremy, red-faced and wearing a white shirt and a tie, was pushing Freddie.

"He keeps pulling my tie, Mrs. Kleintoch! Tell him to leave my tie alone."

Mrs. Kleintoch walked to the back of the line. With her hand firmly on Freddie's shoulder, she whispered in his ear. Heather looked at Jeremy's tie. It was green with a little horse painted on it, a horse rearing up on its hind legs. It was weird to see Jeremy in something other than his baseball shirts.

Freddie's face clouded over as he listened to his teacher. He crossed his arms in front of him and scowled. His hair was all slicked down and shiny. Mrs. Kleintoch smoothed one of his stray hairs into place. "That's it. Now let's at least stay

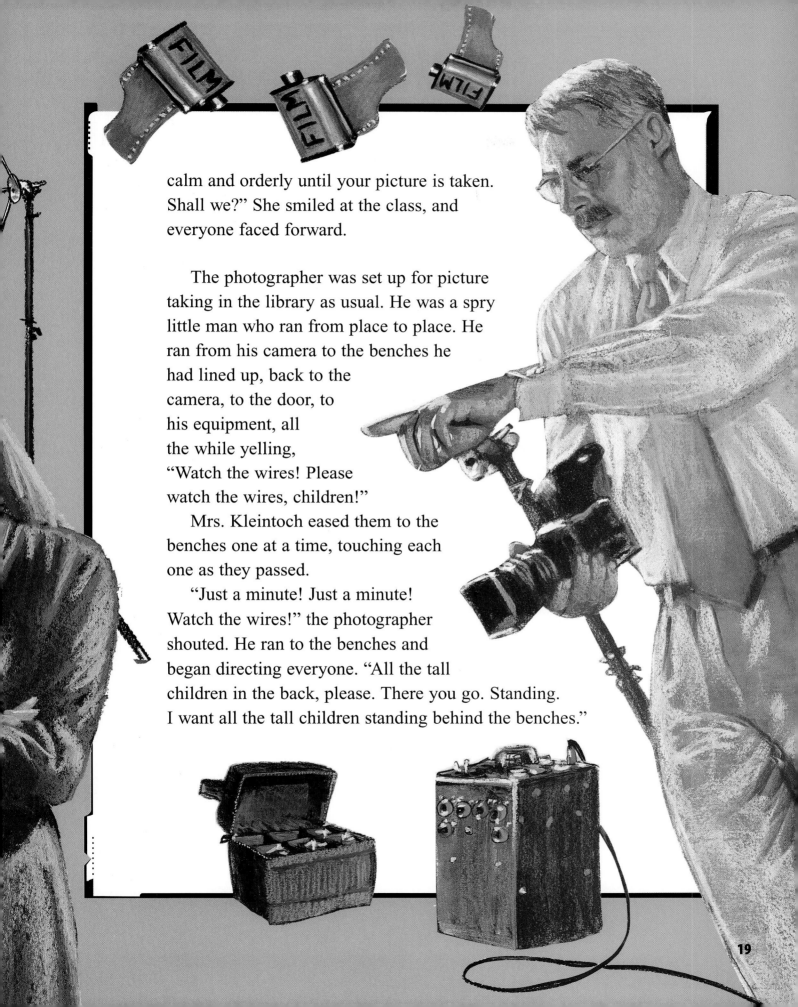

calm and orderly until your picture is taken. Shall we?" She smiled at the class, and everyone faced forward.

The photographer was set up for picture taking in the library as usual. He was a spry little man who ran from place to place. He ran from his camera to the benches he had lined up, back to the camera, to the door, to his equipment, all the while yelling, "Watch the wires! Please watch the wires, children!"

Mrs. Kleintoch eased them to the benches one at a time, touching each one as they passed.

"Just a minute! Just a minute! Watch the wires!" the photographer shouted. He ran to the benches and began directing everyone. "All the tall children in the back, please. There you go. Standing. I want all the tall children standing behind the benches."

He directed and pointed and poked until the whole class was jammed together either behind or on the benches. Heather sat on the first bench next to Sonya. With one foot she felt to make sure her one sock was down, and she pulled the other one up tight.

The photographer peered into his camera at them, and Heather smiled. "Just a minute," he said. "We need some adjustments." First he would peer in the camera and then he would look around at them. "You in the green shirt," he'd say. "Change places with the boy at the end. That's better. That's good. Now you, with the glasses, come in closer."

Heather yawned and just sat there. She glanced at Sonya's clinking beads.

"And you. You in the red sweater."

She wondered how Sonya's mother made such tiny braids like that.

"Heather!" the whole class shouted at once.

Heather was startled.

"Yes, you," the photographer said. "You in the red sweater, I want you to stand in the back next to the boy with the tie."

"But I'm short," she said.

"You're taller than everyone on the bench," he told her, motioning with his arm where to go.

Heather took her place at the end of the back row. She couldn't believe it. Standing in the back row! She wasn't tall enough for the back row, and nobody would see her socks from back here.

The photographer ran to his camera and peered inside once again. "Beautiful," he said. "Now I want everyone to say 'Frank Sinatra.'"

There was dead silence except for Mrs. Kleintoch, who sang right out. "Frank Sinatra."

And when everyone laughed, the photographer snapped the picture.

MRS. KLEINTOCH'S CLASS GRADE 5

THE INSIDE STORY:

How much taller are you this year than last year? You can thank your bones for those extra inches. You're growing taller because your bones are growing longer. These X rays show how the bones in a person's hand grow. How are the X rays different?

INFANT

2-YEAR-OLD

At first, your tiny skeleton was made of a tough, rubbery material called *cartilage*. (Your nose and your ear are still made of cartilage.) Slowly, strong, hard bone began to replace cartilage in your skeleton. The bright white parts in this X ray show where bone has begun to grow.

Just how do your bones grow? At the ends of a bone are areas called *growth plates*. These plates keep forming new cartilage which makes the bone longer. Then bone cells move in to replace the cartilage and make it harder.

SCIENCE FACTS ABOUT
GROWING UP

5-YEAR-OLD

By age 5, more bones in the hand have formed. Others are still growing longer. As bones grow, things happen inside them, too. Slowly a hole forms inside the bone. *Bone marrow* fills this hole. That's where your body makes blood and stores fat.

12-YEAR-OLD

By age 12, almost all of the 30 bones in the hand are in place. The bones will keep growing longer until about age 18. Some cartilage will stay at the ends of the bones near the joints. This makes a cushion between the bones.

Jerry Spinelli's

Tales of a FOURTH GRADE

Rat

AWARD WINNING

Author

Jerry Spinelli

In *Fourth Grade Rats* Jerry Spinelli writes about a boy who isn't sure he's ready for the fourth grade. Spinelli admits he's had some growing pains of his own. Here, the author tells some tales from his own life as a fourth grade rat.

Fourth Grade Heartache

I was in fourth grade when Judy Brooks broke up with me. Judy was my neighbor. She lived up the street at 718 George Street in Norristown, Pennsylvania, where I grew up. As a matter of fact, George Street is Oriole Street in a few of my books, and Norristown is the town of Two Mills in *Maniac Magee, Dump Days,* and *The Bathwater Gang.*

Judy and I were an item for about four years. Then in the fourth grade she informed me that she hated all boys—and that included me. Well, I told her that if that was the case, then I hated all girls. For the next year or two I was into a pretty severe girl-hating stage. By the way, in *Fourth Grade Rats* the girl in the book that the boy really likes is named Judy Billings. She just happens to have the same first name and same initials as Judy Brooks!

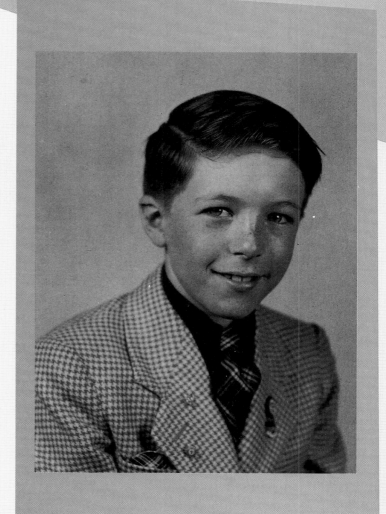

This is me in fourth grade, the year Judy Brooks broke up with me. Can you imagine any girl dumping such a cute little face?

Neighbors

On summer evenings my father and I would go out after dinner and toss a baseball because I wanted to be a Major League shortstop. The Seeton's house was perpendicular to ours—their dining room windows faced our backyard. One evening, my father and I were throwing the ball, and my aim wasn't too accurate. I threw the ball over my father's head right through the Seeton's dining room window. I was a real coward at times like that, so it was up to my father to tell the Seetons what had happened, and offer to pay for it.

After a week or so, the window was fixed. But then a couple of days later my father and I were playing catch again and I did the same thing! It's just unbelievable—same window, same baseball— and my father took care of it again. And the most amazing thing about the whole episode was that none of the Seetons ever said anything about it. Mr. Seeton may have been fuming behind the walls of his own house, but he never said anything to me. I just got off scott free—all I had to deal with was my own conscience.

Overnight Fright

I had two best friends in the fourth grade—Roger Adelman and Johnny Seeton, and I have a little story about each of those friends. My Roger Adelman story makes me cringe, even today, to think of what a baby I was. You see, I was never one to go to camp for weeks at a time or even overnight. I went to YMCA day camp, but I never stayed overnight. To me that seemed too adult. But Roger Adelman went away to Boy Scout camp for a week or two at a time.

Even though I wasn't the type to do this, somehow I ended up with a pup tent. I put it up in my yard and the next thing I knew, I was inviting Roger Adelman to come down and sleep over. So he came down and my mother, as mothers will do, had all kinds of comforts—blankets and snacks and some kind of lantern light. So we had our snacks and chatted and played cards, and then turned out the light and lay down in the pup tent. Roger went to sleep immediately like a veteran Boy Scout. But I was wide awake, nervous and spooked for about an hour or so. Finally, I shook Roger's shoulder to tell him that I had to go back in the house. My last memory is of me picking up my blanket and heading in the back door of my house while Roger trudged off the three or four blocks to his house.

You are looking at the 1953 50-yard dash champion of the Norristown, Pennsylvania, grade schools. Wisely, I retired from track after that.

Adventure at the Creek

Another day I was down at the creek with Johnny Seeton. I had been standing in the water, which was only about a foot deep. When I came up out of the creek I saw that there were leeches—what we used to call bloodsuckers—all over my shins. Well, I knew what to do in case of rattlesnake bite from reading books and watching movies. You'd just get out your old trusty knife, make an X-shaped cut at the bite mark, and suck out the poison. So I figured, well, I guess you do something similar for leeches. I must have thought they were poisonous. So I brushed the leeches off my legs—I did not have the nerve to start making cuts—and I told Johnny to start sucking. The last thing I remember was a kid with horror in his eyes turning and running and racing up the steep bank, and that was the last of Johnny that I saw that afternoon. And I went with wet shins and bare feet to my house wondering if I was going to die in a few days because my friend wouldn't suck out the poison.

A Happy Ending

I want to end by saying that in spite of some unpleasant memories, fourth grade wasn't all bad. In fact, one of the best things I remember from that time is my teacher, Miss Coleman. As the years go by, I tend to appreciate her more and more. That's why I dedicated my book *Fourth Grade Rats* to her.

Here I am having lunch at a school I visited. As you can see, I'll do anything for a free lunch—even eat with kids.

I had <u>two</u> best friends in the fourth grade. Here's a poem I wrote about the situation.

Stuck

In fourth grade
for some reason we had
this test
and one of the questions was:
<u>Who is your best friend?</u>
I was really stuck
because I could not decide
between Roger Adelman
who was in my class
and Johnny Seeton
who was my neighbor.
Surely the one I didn't choose
would be offended.
The answer space
was still a blank
when the teacher called
for papers.
Quickly,
I wrote in both names.
I never found out
how well I did.

—Jerry Spinelli

Jerry Spinelli

JOHN·NEWBERY·MEDAL

FOR THE
MOST DISTINGUISHED
CONTRIBUTION
TO
AMERICAN LITERATURE
FOR CHILDREN

**JERRY SPINELLI
1991**

Author

Authors are *full* of the *"write"* stuff.

As an author of children's books, Jerry Spinelli is so successful that writing is his full-time job. But he never thought much about writing when he was growing up. "My dream was to play baseball. I was going to be a shortstop in the major leagues."

PROFILE

Name: Jerry Spinelli

Occupation: author

Pets: a rat named Daisy and Chi-Chi the chinchilla

Favorite thing to read: Bugs Bunny comics

Book that won the Newbery Medal: *Maniac Magee*

Special skills: flipping baseball cards

QUESTIONS

for Jerry Spinelli

Discover how **Jerry Spinelli** became a **writer.**

Q **What made you decide to become a writer instead of a baseball player?**

A When I was sixteen my high school football team won a big game. I was so excited—I wrote a poem about it. A local newspaper published the poem. That's when I decided to become a writer.

Q **And how did you become a writer?**

A Well, first I became a grown-up. And I thought, *Now on to the important stuff!* So I tried writing grown-up novels about important stuff. But nobody wanted to publish them.

Q **What made you decide to try children's books?**

A I married my wife Eileen, a writer who already had five kids. One night, one of our little angels snuck into the refrigerator and swiped a piece of fried chicken I was saving for lunch. When I discovered the chicken was gone, I wrote about it. That piece of writing became my first published novel, *Space Station Seventh Grade*. At the time I had no idea I was going to write a children's book.

Do you have a regular writing schedule?

 I usually write in the morning from 10:00 to noon. Then after dinner, I write some more from 9:00 to midnight. I like working at night.

 Are your childhood memories important to your writing?

When I was growing up, I didn't think my childhood was special. It was full of kid stuff: bike riding, flipping baseball cards, and catching poison ivy. It wasn't until I started writing about it that I realized what an adventure it had been!

 What do you like best about your job?

The best part is being able to make a living from what I do. I was able to quit my job as an editor of a magazine. I love writing, and the fact that I get paid for it is an added bonus.

Jerry Spinelli's Tips for Young Writers

1. **Subject Matter:** See how successful authors write for themselves as well as for their audience.

2. **Trust Your Ideas:** Remember to listen to your ideas.

3. **Keep Writing:** Whether playing the piano, baseball, or writing, the more you do something, the more you will improve. Have fun with it!

How to
Create a Table of Contents

The title of the chapter describes what the chapter is about.

When you pick up a book, how can you tell what the story is about? One way is to read the Table of Contents.

What is a Table of Contents? The Table of Contents is a list of the chapter titles you will find in a book. Sometimes, you can tell if you will like a book just by reading the titles of the chapters. Chapters with interesting titles will grab the reader's attention.

> The word *Contents* goes at the top of the page.

Contents

> The page number gives the page on which the chapter begins.

> One way to organize chapters is by putting them in the order that the events happened.

1 Choose Events From Your Life

List all the important events you can remember from your life. Here are some ideas to help get you started. Did you ever take a fun trip? make a new friend? win an award? move to another city? Are there photographs of special moments from your life? Make a list of events, and choose at least six of your favorite ones. These will be the chapters in your Table of Contents.

TOOLS

- pencil and paper
- colored markers
- photographs of your life

2 Create Chapter Titles

Once you have your list of possible chapters, the next step is to give them titles. Keep in mind that a title gives the reader an idea of what that chapter is about. Look at your list of events, and think about how each one makes you feel. If one of the events is funny, give it a funny title. Use lots of action words and descriptive details to add life to your titles.

3 Organize Your Table of Contents

After choosing your chapter titles, think about how to organize them in your Table of Contents. You could list them in chronological order, or divide them into different categories. One chapter might be about family, another about sports, and still another about school.

Tip Try reading your titles to some friends and ask them what they think the chapters will be about.

4 Put It All Together

Make up a title for your book and write it at the top of the page. Underneath the title write *Table of Contents,* then list your chapter titles. Finish your Table of Contents by adding made-up page numbers. Then share your work with your classmates.

If You Are Using a Computer ...

Write a short journal entry for each event that you want to include in your Table of Contents. Make up a title for each entry, and then print them out. After looking at them, decide on their order, and use the titles to write your Table of Contents.

FIRST PLACE

THINK

Imagine that you are ten years older. What new chapter titles might you add to your Table of Contents?

Jerry Spinelli
Author ▶

With a Little Help

Meet an Appalachian girl who teaches her classmates about courage.

Laugh with Rudy as he practices party etiquette with his dad. Then read a humorous advice column.

WORKSHOP 2

Make a book jacket starring *you*.

When I Was Nine
by James Stevenson

The Rag Coat

by Lauren Mills

In winter, Papa carried me to church in a burlap feed sack because I didn't have a coat. Mama, Papa, Clemmie, and me—we'd all hitch a ride on Jeremy Miller's hay wagon and huddle under Mama's big quilt. I know Papa loved that quilt, because he said it had all the nice, bright colors of the day in it, and the day was something he hardly ever saw. He worked down in the black coal mines and didn't come up till the sun was gone.

I told Papa it was warmer under that quilt than if I *had* a coat. He always laughed when I said that, and told me, "Minna, you got the right way of thinking. People only need people, and nothing else. Don't you forget that."

Papa got sick with the miner's cough and couldn't work much, so Mama stitched day and night on her quilts to try to make some money.

When I was old enough to start school, I couldn't go. They needed me at home to help Mama. I would card all her quilt stuffing and keep Clemmie's dirty fingers out of all that cotton. I made a doll for myself by stitching up some of Mama's quilt scraps and stuffing cotton inside. I talked to her like she was my friend, because I didn't have any. Mama was too busy for much talk, and when Papa was home he mostly stared out the window.

The summer I was eight, Papa called me over to his rocking chair. I climbed up on his lap and he said, "You're getting big, Minna."

"Too big for laps?" I asked.

"Not too big for mine," he said softly, "but too big to still be at home. It's nearing time you went to school."

I could hardly hold back my smiling just thinking about all the friends I would have. But I didn't want to leave Mama without a helper. "Papa," I said, "I can't go to school. Mama needs me here."

Papa just looked at me real steady and said, "They have books at school, Minna. You can learn things from those books that you can't learn at home."

"But I don't have a coat, Papa," I quietly reminded him.

"Minna," he said, "don't you worry about a coat. I'll think of something." But he never got the chance. Papa died that summer.

Everyone came at once and brought us food. I couldn't figure out how so many people could squeeze into our little cabin, but somehow they managed it. They all said they knew my papa well.

I sat on a stool back by the woodstove with Clemmie on my lap, so no one would step on us.

I couldn't stand it! They all wore black, black like the coal mines that killed my papa. He didn't even like black. He liked all the bright colors of the day. So why were they wearing black, I wondered.

School started in September. Mama said I could go, but I decided not to. I still didn't have a coat to wear, and I knew it was no use starting something I'd have to quit when the weather turned cold.

Other mothers who had children in school came over to quilt with Mama. I called them the Quilting Mothers. That fall they were all working on a pattern called Joseph's Coat of Many Colors. I looked at it and said, "That Joseph sure was lucky to have such a coat. I wish I had one like that."

"Why do you say that, Minna?" Mrs. Miller asked me.

"Because then I could go to school," I said, a little embarrassed that I had mentioned it.

"Well now, Minna," said Mrs. Miller, "I don't know that any of us has a spare coat we could hand down to you, but I'm sure we have some scraps to spare. We could piece them together, and you'd have a coat like Joseph's after all." Mrs. Miller looked around the room, and the other mothers nodded.

Mama quickly protested. "You all need those rags for your own quilts. Don't go giving us things you need yourselves."

They paid no attention to Mama. Mrs. Hunter said, "And we could use feed bags for the inside of the coat."

My eyes filled with tears, but I wasn't embarrassed anymore. I said, "I have a feed sack Papa used to carry me in!" I ran and fetched it. "Will this do?"

Yes, it would do just fine, they told me. Then I thought of something important. "But you need to make quilts to *sell*. You can't take time out to quilt a coat."

"First things first," said Mrs. Miller, and they all repeated it. Mama smiled and shook her head, and I saw tears in her eyes, too.

The very next day I went to school, running most of
the way to keep warm and thinking all the while of the coat
I would soon have.

The schoolhouse was just one room filled with fourteen
children. I had seen most of them at church but never got
the chance to talk to them much.

I knew I would love school, even though I was put in
the front row with the youngest ones, and Clyde Bradshaw
whispered that it was because I was dumb. Then Shane
Hunter pulled my braid, and Souci Miller said I asked
the teacher too many questions. But our teacher, Miss
Campbell, smiled at me and said, "Smart people are those
who have asked a lot of questions."

My most favorite thing about school was Sharing Day.
Each of us had our own day when we shared something
special with the class.

Clyde Bradshaw brought in the watch his grandpa
gave him. It still ticked, and he made sure we all heard it.

On her day Lottie showed us the porcelain doll her aunt from New York had sent her. We all thought it was the most beautiful thing ever and wanted to touch it, but Lottie wouldn't let anyone near it. She said, "Nope, it's mine," which made everybody mad.

I knew just what I would show when it was my Sharing Day, but I kept it a secret, and I knew the Quilting Mothers would keep it a secret, too.

Each day I hurried home to see my coat. It was looking like the colors of the fall days—the yellow-golds of the birch leaves, the silvery grays and purples of the sky, the deep greens and browns of the pines, and the rusty reds of the chimney bricks—all the colors Papa would have chosen. I decided to put a piece of his work jacket in there. It just seemed right.

The mothers worked as quickly as they could, but the cold weather was quicker. At recess Souci asked me why I didn't wear a coat. I told her I couldn't jump rope as well with one on. Jumping a lot kept me warm. I was fast becoming the best rope-jumper in the school.

Not last night but the night before
Twenty-four robbers came knocking at my door.

That was my favorite rope tune.

One night when Mama looked sad I told her things could be worse. We could have twenty-four robbers knocking at our door.

She said, "Now, what on earth would they want from *us*, Minna?"

"Oh, Mama, they would want the coat, first thing," I said.

She laughed then, but I was most serious.

Finally my coat was done. It was so beautiful, and the Quilting Mothers had finished it in time for my Sharing Day!

That morning I walked to school looking down at all the different colored pieces of cloth in my coat. All the stories the Quilting Mothers had told me about the rags and who they belonged to, I knew by heart. I had ended up choosing the most worn pieces for my coat because the best stories went with them. I was still looking down and repeating each story to myself when I bumped into Clyde outside the schoolyard.

"Hey, Rag-Coat!" he said, and all the others laughed. Before I knew it, Souci, Lottie, and Clyde were dancing around me singing, "Rag-Coat! Rag-Coat!"

Lottie said, "Look, it's even dirty with soot!" and she poked her finger into my papa's cloth!

Then Souci said, "Hey, Minna, you were better off with *no* coat than with that old, ragged thing."

"Maybe you're right!" I yelled. "If I had *no* coat, then I never would have come to school!" I broke through their circle and ran away from them, far into the woods.

I found an old log and sat on it for a long time, too angry to cry. I just stared across the fields Papa used to gaze at.

"Oh, Papa, I wish you were here," I said, and then I couldn't help but cry. I cried for Papa, and I cried for the Quilting Mothers, who had wasted their time. I was crying so hard I rocked that old log.

Then all at once I stopped because I felt something warm and familiar. The feed bag inside my coat made me feel like Papa's arms were around me again. I could almost hear him say, "Minna, people only need people, and nothing else. Don't you forget that."

I jumped off the log, wiped the tears from my cheeks, and brushed the leaves off my coat. "I won't forget it, Papa," I said, and I headed back to school.

When I walked into the schoolroom, Miss Campbell looked up, surprised. "Why, Minna," she said, "I was told you ran home sick."

Souci jumped up, her face all red. "That's not true, Miss Campbell," she blurted out. "We lied to you. Minna left because we made fun of her old coat."

"I'll tell her, Souci," I said. "It's not an *old* coat. It's a *new* coat."

"But it's just a bunch of old rags," said Lottie.

"It is not just a bunch of old rags!" I said. "My coat is full of stories, stories about everybody here."

They all looked at me, real puzzled.

"Don't you see? These are all *your* rags!" They still seemed puzzled.

So I showed them. "Look, Shane, here is that blanket of yours that your mama's sister gave her the night you were born. The midwife said you wouldn't live but three days because you were so small. But your mama wrapped you up tight in that blanket and put you in a little box by the woodstove. And your papa kept the fire all night for three weeks. Of course, you lived, all right," I said, looking up at Shane. Shane was big. "And you hung on to that blanket for years, until it was nothing but shreds."

"My blanket," he whispered. "I thought I'd *never* see it again." He looked at his old rag like he wanted to touch it.

Then the others began discovering their old, favorite things and crowded around me. They each wanted their story told, and I remembered every one.

I even showed the piece of the woolen jacket Souci had let her calf wear when it was sick. Lottie's rag was a faded piece from the fancy dress her aunt from New York had sent for her seventh birthday. And Clyde had a scrap from the pants that he always wore when he went fishing with his grandpa.

Souci said, "Minna, I sure am sorry we ever said anything bad about your coat."

"Me, too," I heard the others murmur.

"I wouldn't blame you if you didn't let us touch it," Lottie said.

"I wouldn't blame you if you didn't want to be our friend at all!" said Clyde.

"Friends share," I said, and I let them each touch their rag. Then I showed them the feed sack inside my coat and told them how it made me feel my papa's arms again.

Shane put his hand on my shoulder and said, "Minna, I bet you got the warmest coat in school."

"Well, it took a *whole lot of people* to make it warm," I told him, and we all laughed.

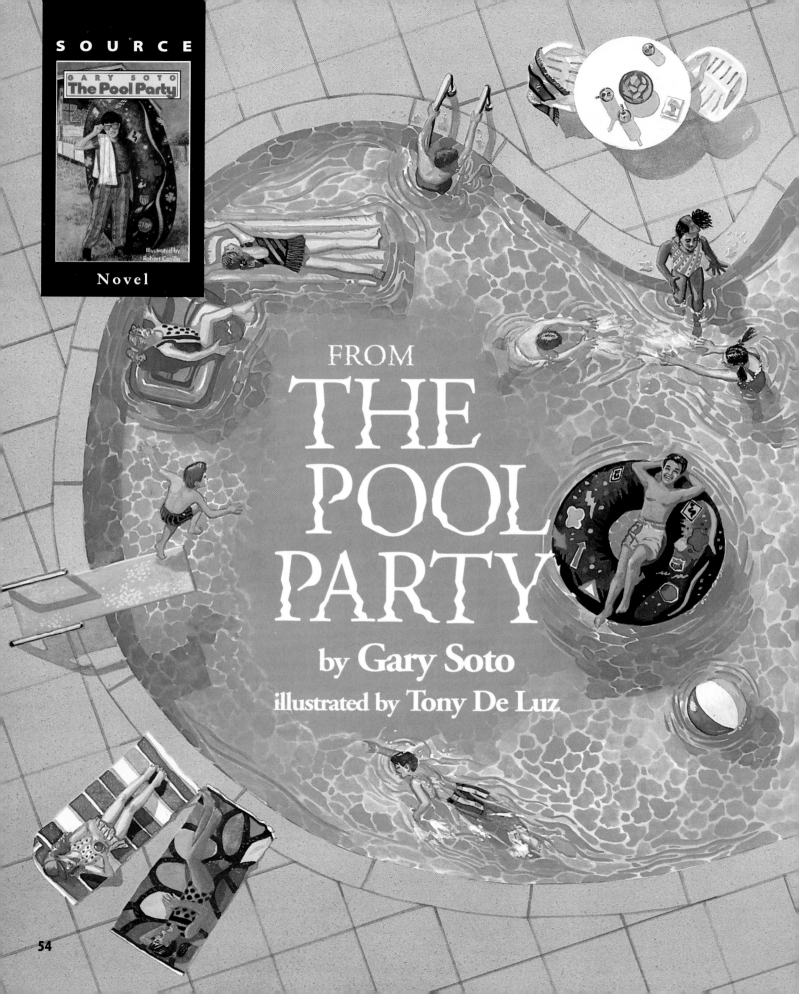

GARY SOTO
The Pool Party

Illustrated by
Robert Casilla

FROM

THE POOL PARTY

by **Gary Soto**

illustrated by **Tony De Luz**

The morning sun blazed above the roofs of the neighborhood. And although it was still morning, the little kids from across the street were already running through the sprinklers. Rudy was on the porch bouncing a fluorescent tennis ball against the wall. Father came out, coffee cup in hand. He blew on his coffee and took a sip.

"It's going to be a hot one," he said. His glasses glinted with the sun. His brow was furrowed from squinting at the glare on the street.

"I don't care how hot it gets," Rudy said. He stuffed the ball into his pocket. "I'm going swimming."

Rudy had talked up a storm about the party. He had talked about his inner tube and about Tiffany Perez, the girl in his class. He talked about what he was going to wear and what kinds of dives he would do in the swimming pool. He had told Alex that he was going to try to hold his breath underwater for two minutes.

"Sit down, Little Rudy," Father said. He took a sip of coffee and looked thoughtfully at the sky. "So Tiffany is pretty rich, huh?"

"I think so."

"Well, Rudy, let me give you some advice. You can't eat with your fingers."

"Yeah, I know," Rudy said. "Estela told me already."

"And when you get there, you gotta be polite. You have to make small talk."

"Small talk?"

"Yeah, you got to talk so small that ants can understand what you're saying." He rubbed his chin and thought deeply.

"Let me help you. I'll be
Mrs. Perez and you be yourself."

"You're going to be Mrs. Perez?"

"*Simón.*"

They stood up, face-to-face. Rudy pretended to
knock on the door.

"How's it going, ma'am?" Rudy said as he greeted
Mrs. Perez. He had a difficult time seeing Mrs. Perez in the
form of his father, especially in a work shirt and thick
black glasses.

"No, Rudy. You have to be polite," Father corrected
him. "Say, 'Hello, Mrs. Perez. It's a swell day for a swell
pool party.' Can you do that? And immediately start making
conversation. You could tell her about yourself. Tell her
about baseball."

Rudy tried a second time. He knocked and said, "Hello,
Mrs. Perez, it's sure a hot day for a hot pool party. I adore
fried chicken."

"That's it, *hombre,*" Father screamed with delight.
He slapped his thighs and said, "Tell her more. *Otra vez.*"

"I adore fried chicken *con frijoles,* and *mi perro,*
Chorizo, he likes tortillas with peanut butter." Rudy giggled
and slapped his own thighs.

"That's it, Rudy," Father encouraged. "Tell her more.
Spit it out!"

"I like *huevos con weenies y papas fritas. Me gustan café
con leche y helado de coco.*" Rudy was smiling from ear to
ear as he realized how funny he sounded. He reminded
himself of Kid Frost, the rapper from East Los Angeles.

Father slapped his thighs a second time. He took a sip from his coffee cup and smiled broadly at his son. "Rudy, you're gonna be a hit. Bethany-Tiffany-Riffany, or whatever her name is, she's gonna crack up. You know why?"

"No. Why, Dad?"

"You mean you don't know why?"

"No, Dad. Why?"

Father became more serious. "Sit down, Little Rudy." He popped his knuckles and looked around the neighborhood. More children were playing in the sprinklers. The neighbor across the street was washing her car.

"Rudy, we're just ordinary *gente*," Father started. "I work, and El Shorty—your gramps—works. We get by. We're honest. That's it. We get by month to month. That's why she's gonna like you. She's gonna see that you're real. *¿Entiendes?*" He stopped and waved to a neighbor driving past. "Hey, Louie, I got that jack for you. Come by later." The man in the car waved and nodded his head. Father looked at his son with understanding. "Listen, they may be rich folks, but don't worry. Just go and have fun, do some fancy dives in the pool and be nice and . . . bring me home a piece of cake. Okay?"

"Okay, Dad," Rudy said. He understood his father. He understood that while they were everyday workers, they were proud and worked as one—*la familia*. He understood that his father was a good father, serious but not too serious.

Father left with Grandfather to cut lawns. Rudy played with Chorizo and then, struck with a little guilt, he stopped to admire his grandfather's landscaping efforts. His grandfather was working on making a pool in their own backyard. "*Pobre abuelito*," thought Rudy, "I should help him." Rudy shoveled until he was hot and sweaty and it was time to go to the pool party.

He showered and then, at the foggy bathroom mirror, practiced making polite conversation. "Hello, Mrs. Perez, I adore fried chicken." He raised two splayed fingers and said, "I'll take two pieces." He splashed his father's cologne on his face. "It's a hot day for a swell pool party." He splashed on more cologne. He admired himself in the mirror. "Mrs. Perez," he continued, "I understand that you love turtle soup. I, too, adore turtle soup." He was happy with his small talk, and happy with the way he smelled.

When he came into the kitchen, where Mother was ironing his shirt, he said in a British accent, "Hello, dear mother. I must be off for the pool party."

"Oh, you look so handsome," she said. She pulled at his cheek and said, "*¡Qué bonito!*"

"Mom, I'm ten years old. I'm not a baby."

"You're my baby." She beamed. She had never seen her son so clean, and so dressed up. She sniffed the air. She studied her son with a little smile on her face.

"You smell nice, like your *papi*," she said as she handed him the ironed shirt.

"Well"—he blushed—"I put on a little bit of his cologne."

Mother smiled and asked, "You have a ride?"

"*Simón,*" Rudy said, snapping his fingers. "I got my own wheels, Mom. My inner tube!"

Rudy's ride was his inner tube—taller than his father and wide as Alex. He left the house and rolled it up the street, past the neighbor kids who were once again in the sprinklers. Past his sister who was sitting on a car fender dreaming about boys. Past Louie the neighbor and his dog Charlie. Past other dogs and mothers and the lawns browning under the Fresno sun. A mile north, where the houses turned nice, he passed it all, including his father and El Shorty, whom he didn't see. Their Oldsmobile was stalled. They had run over a board with a nail and now had a flat tire. He didn't hear them scream, "Hey, Little Rudy, we need that inner tube!"

He had on sunglasses, and his headset on his ears, listening to Kid Frost. Father and El Shorty called and shouted, "Little Rudy, come back!" But Rudy rolled his inner tube toward the pool party, rehearsing inside his head, "Hello, Mrs. Perez, I adore fried chicken."

From

PENNY POLLARD'S GUIDE TO MODERN MANNERS

by Robin Klein

Penny Pollard's school assignment is to write a report on good manners. Penny soon becomes a pro at politeness. She even starts an advice column for kids who have questions about etiquette.

 peechless

Dear Trouble Shooter

I was asked out to lunch and the hostess served with pride and joy a totally horrible mucky mixture of squid, lima beans and onions in horse radish sauce. I just took one mouthful and gagged! How can I handle it if I get asked over there again?

Poisoned

Dear Poisoned

Unfortunately you'll have to eat a little bit (though you might be lucky enough to have an allergy to some of the ingredients and can truthfully say so).

Take small mouthfuls and sips of water. When the plates are being collected and it becomes obvious you've left most of your helping, say, 'It was really delicious, but I made the mistake of having a huge late breakfast.' Or, 'I hate not being able to finish this when you went to so much trouble, but I've got a tiny appetite and I want to leave room for that yummy-looking fermented goat's cheese dessert.' Or (looking really apologetic), 'Creative cooking is just wasted on me, I'm afraid. Mum says my idea of a gourmet meal is a tomato sandwich.' (None of this will fool the hostess for a minute, of course, but at least you're not hurting her feelings.)

Yours faithfully
Trouble Shooter

Double Ducks

Dear Trouble Shooter

On my birthday I unwrapped one of the presents, a terrific umbrella with a carved duck handle. The only trouble was that the last present I'd unwrapped was exactly the same, and both present-givers looked really embarrassed.

Ducky

Dear Ducky

You could have said something like, 'Oh, that's fantastic, getting *two*! Now I'll be able to keep one in my room, and the other one in the car for emergencies.'

Trouble Shooter

P.S. If you happen to know where they were bought, you could take one back to the shop secretly and explain to the shop assistant what happened. They might let you exchange it for something else, but be careful the present-giver doesn't ever suspect.

How to
Make a
Book Jacket

Have you ever picked up a book because you liked the way the cover looked? You can learn a lot about a book from its cover illustration and the information found on the book jacket.

What is a book jacket? A book jacket is made up of several parts. The front cover shows the title of the book, the name of the author, and artwork related to the book. The inside front flap has a paragraph about the book, while the back cover may have quotes from reviewers or a photo of the author.

The title is on the cover.

The author's name is below the title.

When I Was Nine
by James Stevenson

My own children are grown up now; that's how old I am. But sometimes I look back and I remember . . .

In that pre-World War II time, the radios were bigger, the cars larger, and the days seemed to be longer. But some things were exactly as they are now: arithmetic, older brothers, and the ecstasy of jumping into an icy mountain stream. This evocation of a summer in the 1930s is the perfect answer for every grandchild (and child) who has ever said, "Tell me about when you were little."

The inside flap gives a summary of the book.

Pictures give clues to what the book is about.

1 Brainstorm

What words and pictures tell a story about you? Get out your notebook and jot down things you like to do, places you like to go, people you know, talents you have, and all the words you can think of that tell about you.

TOOLS

- pencil and ruler
- construction paper
- colored markers
- picture of you
- glue

My best friend

2 Investigate

When you've finished your list, put check marks next to your best ideas. Decide on a title for your book. Then look at some book jackets to see what pictures, titles, and designs they use. Write down some ideas for your own jacket design. Think about what colors you want to use and what pictures should go on your cover.

My family's trip to Chicago

My winning goal that won the soccer game

3 Write Flap Copy

After deciding on a cover design, the next step is to write a brief paragraph that describes what your book is about. This paragraph is like a short book report. It goes inside the front flap of your book cover and is called flap copy. The more interesting the flap copy, the more likely that people will read your book. Be sure to use lots of details when you write your paragraph.

Tips
- Having trouble drawing? Try using some family photos—but ask first! Or use some pictures from magazines and make a collage.
- Don't be afraid to use lots of bright colors. Remember, a book jacket has to catch your eye!

The first time I rode a bicycle

The time that the dog ate my birthday cake

4 Make Your Book Jacket

- Fold a piece of construction paper in half to make the jacket. Then fold down the inside flaps.
- Draw the design you want on the cover, and then add the title and your name.
- Put your flap copy on the inside of the front flap.
- If you want, decorate the back cover with a picture of yourself or some "quotes" from made-up book reviews.

If You Are Using a Computer ...

Create your book cover on the computer. You can choose a border that you like and clip art that tells about you. After you've decided on what to call your book, type the title and your name with a special font.

THINK
How do you think famous people choose what to put in their autobiographies?

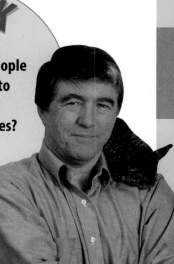
Jerry Spinelli
Author ▶

Augustin
Bad Homburg
von der Höhe
1970

Families and traditions are an important part of who we are.

A Pocketful of Memories

Listen as a father tells how he met Eleanor Roosevelt. Afterward, meet another First Lady.

Take a tour of a young Cherokee girl's world.

Learn about an artist's childhood through her words and paintings.

PROJECT

Turn a favorite memory into a personal narrative.

S O U R C E

FRONT PORCH
STORIES
at the One-Room School

Eleanora E. Tate
author of *Thank You, Dr. Martin Luther King Jr.!*
Illustrated by Eric Velasquez

Short
Stories

From
FRONT PORCH STORIES
at the One-Room School
by **Eleanora E. Tate**
illustrated by **Eric Velasquez**

THE

AWARD WINNING

Author

One hot summer night, 12-year-old Margie Carson and her cousin Ethel picnic on the old school's front porch with Margie's dad. He tells them stories about the childhood adventures he shared with his sister Stella and their twin cousins, Delmo and Elmo.

Daddy yawned. "But hey, the wife of a United States president came here one time."

"You mean, the one who has that dog that wrote a book?" asked Ethel.

"No, that's somebody else. I mean, Eleanor Roosevelt, wife of Franklin Roosevelt. She was probably the most famous of all the presidents' wives. She was a good friend to Dr. Mary McLeod Bethune, too, who was an internationally known educator and leader."

"Well, come on and tell us about when Mrs. Roosevelt came," I said.

On this particular Sunday afternoon, Elmo, Delmo, Stella, and I were up here playing soccer, Daddy began. Delmo and I played against Stella and Elmo. I lined the ball up level with the edge of the old log cabin that used to set in the park area behind the school, near the highway. That was our goal line to defend.

The edge of the schoolhouse was the goal line for Stella and Elmo to defend. The object of the game was to beat up the other team and kick the ball over their goal line at the same time.

We couldn't play *too* rough, because if Stella got hurt it would be my fault. You know how that goes with little kids.

I kicked the ball hard over Stella's head to start us off. It landed just in front of my partner Delmo who guided it with quick little kicks toward the schoolhouse. Elmo, Stella's goalie, was back there waiting on him.

I followed behind, to be on hand to help and to protect our goal line at the same time.

Suddenly Elmo whizzed past Delmo and tripped him. Delmo went flat on his back while Elmo made off with the ball.

"Cheat! No fair!" I yelled. I flew into Elmo and tried to tangle up his feet with mine and get the ball away. But Elmo kicked the ball around to Stella, who galloped up the yard toward the log cabin.

I had almost caught up with her when Elmo banged into me and knocked me flat. I saw stars. By the time I got up, Delmo was hobbling after Stella. He caught up with her and stole the ball away. I raced to the log cabin. Just in time! Elmo stole the ball from Delmo and sliced it over to Stella. She cut loose with her best kick.

The ball popped up in the air and hit the roof of the cabin. I shot around to the other side. If I could catch it before it touched the ground, I could keep them from scoring. If I missed, they'd go ahead of us two to zip.

The ball rolled off the roof, hit a tree, and bounced over my head. I scrambled backwards, trying to catch it before it hit the ground.

"Stop!" everybody hollered, so I did.

And found myself in the middle of the street, with a big white car coming right at me!

Screech! The car stopped not two inches from me. I was so scared, I couldn't even breathe right. That car stopped so hard that it left tire marks on Highway 61 for a month afterwards. But better the road than on me.

"Kid?" A White man jumped out of the car and ran over to me. "Kid, are you okay?" He squatted down in front of me and patted me all over. "Didn't you see me?"

Sanity started to return to my brain. I managed to nod and shake my head.

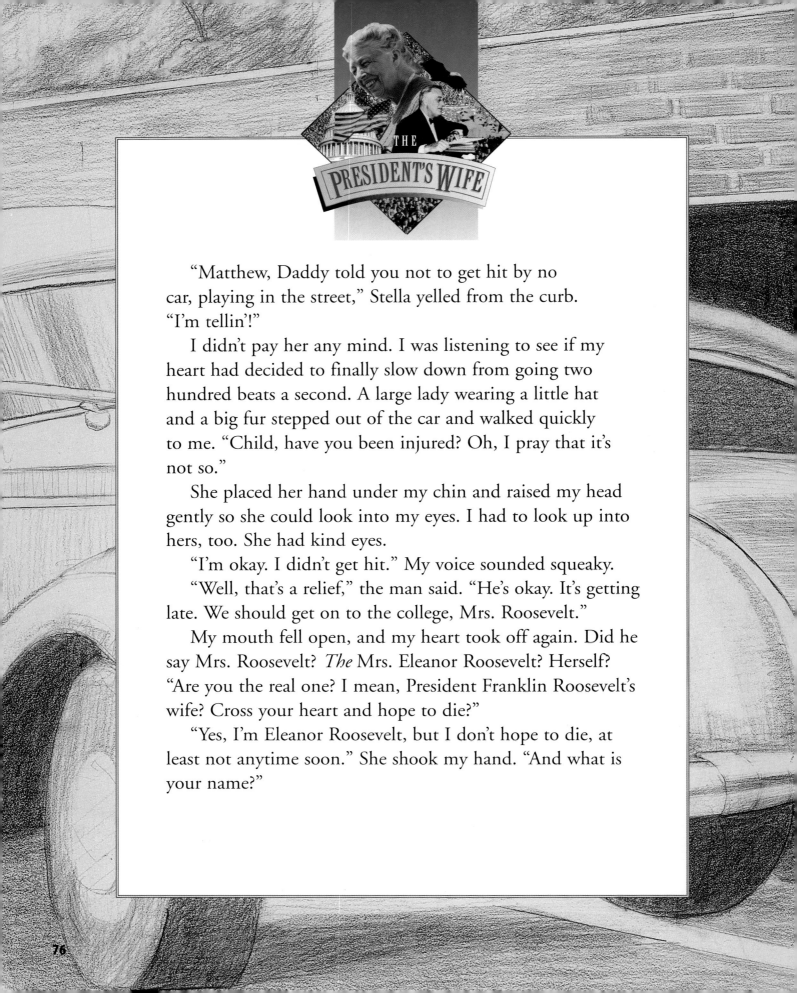

"Matthew, Daddy told you not to get hit by no car, playing in the street," Stella yelled from the curb. "I'm tellin'!"

I didn't pay her any mind. I was listening to see if my heart had decided to finally slow down from going two hundred beats a second. A large lady wearing a little hat and a big fur stepped out of the car and walked quickly to me. "Child, have you been injured? Oh, I pray that it's not so."

She placed her hand under my chin and raised my head gently so she could look into my eyes. I had to look up into hers, too. She had kind eyes.

"I'm okay. I didn't get hit." My voice sounded squeaky.

"Well, that's a relief," the man said. "He's okay. It's getting late. We should get on to the college, Mrs. Roosevelt."

My mouth fell open, and my heart took off again. Did he say Mrs. Roosevelt? *The* Mrs. Eleanor Roosevelt? Herself? "Are you the real one? I mean, President Franklin Roosevelt's wife? Cross your heart and hope to die?"

"Yes, I'm Eleanor Roosevelt, but I don't hope to die, at least not anytime soon." She shook my hand. "And what is your name?"

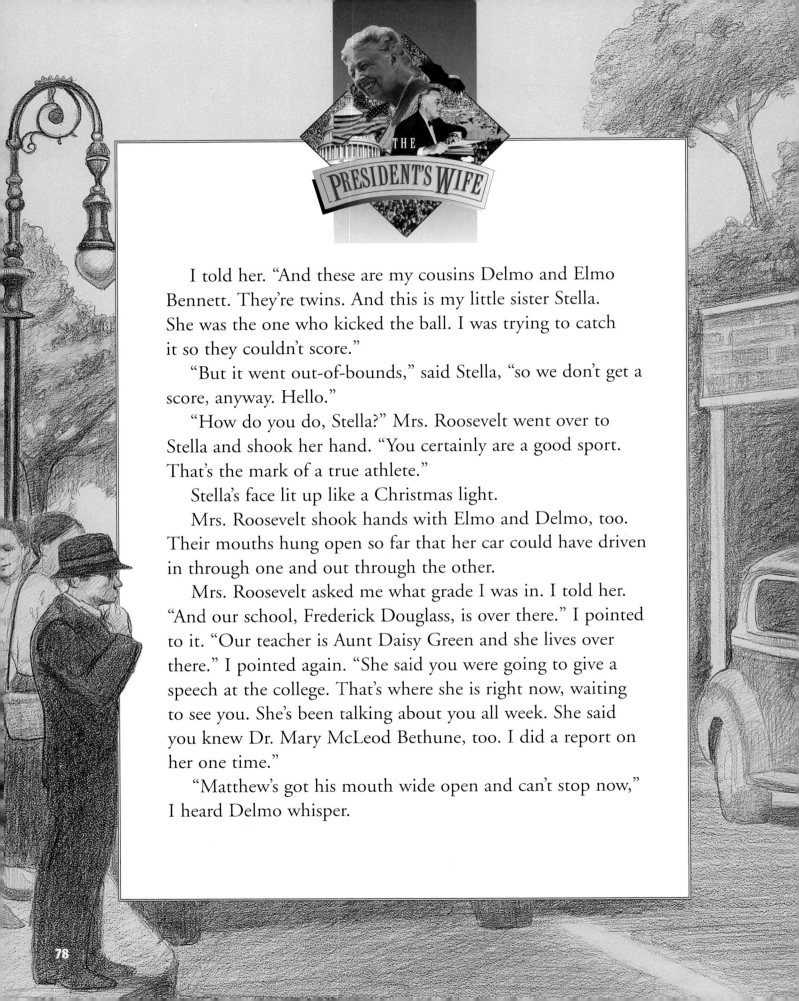

I told her. "And these are my cousins Delmo and Elmo Bennett. They're twins. And this is my little sister Stella. She was the one who kicked the ball. I was trying to catch it so they couldn't score."

"But it went out-of-bounds," said Stella, "so we don't get a score, anyway. Hello."

"How do you do, Stella?" Mrs. Roosevelt went over to Stella and shook her hand. "You certainly are a good sport. That's the mark of a true athlete."

Stella's face lit up like a Christmas light.

Mrs. Roosevelt shook hands with Elmo and Delmo, too. Their mouths hung open so far that her car could have driven in through one and out through the other.

Mrs. Roosevelt asked me what grade I was in. I told her. "And our school, Frederick Douglass, is over there." I pointed to it. "Our teacher is Aunt Daisy Green and she lives over there." I pointed again. "She said you were going to give a speech at the college. That's where she is right now, waiting to see you. She's been talking about you all week. She said you knew Dr. Mary McLeod Bethune, too. I did a report on her one time."

"Matthew's got his mouth wide open and can't stop now," I heard Delmo whisper.

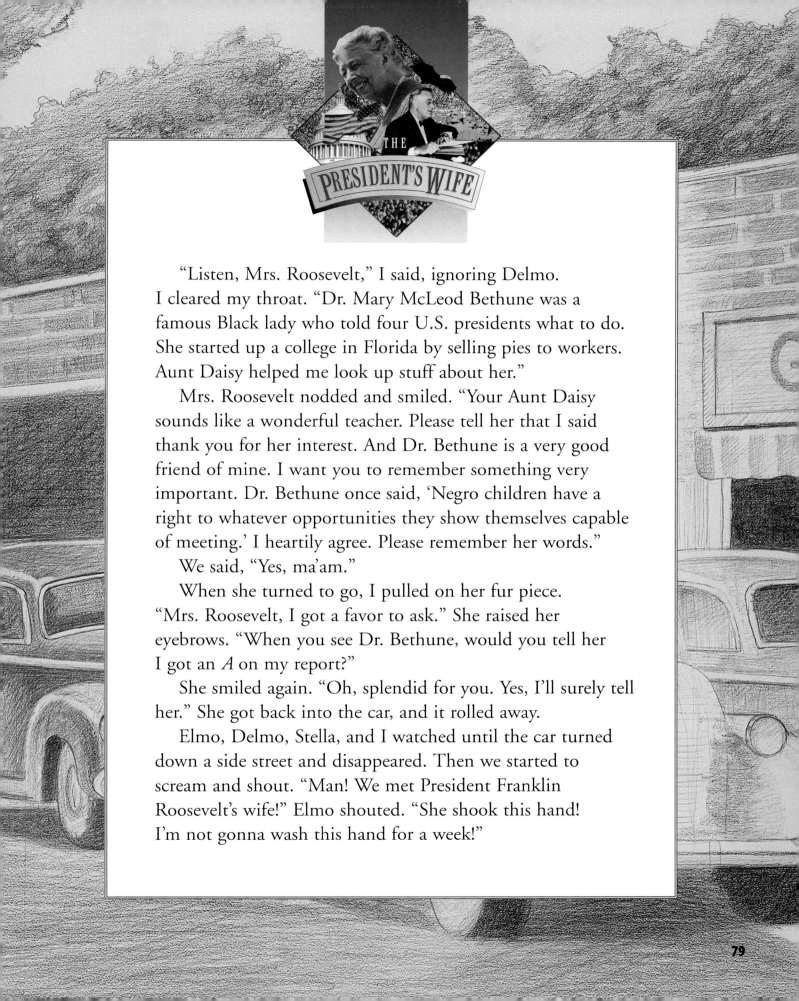

"Listen, Mrs. Roosevelt," I said, ignoring Delmo. I cleared my throat. "Dr. Mary McLeod Bethune was a famous Black lady who told four U.S. presidents what to do. She started up a college in Florida by selling pies to workers. Aunt Daisy helped me look up stuff about her."

Mrs. Roosevelt nodded and smiled. "Your Aunt Daisy sounds like a wonderful teacher. Please tell her that I said thank you for her interest. And Dr. Bethune is a very good friend of mine. I want you to remember something very important. Dr. Bethune once said, 'Negro children have a right to whatever opportunities they show themselves capable of meeting.' I heartily agree. Please remember her words."

We said, "Yes, ma'am."

When she turned to go, I pulled on her fur piece. "Mrs. Roosevelt, I got a favor to ask." She raised her eyebrows. "When you see Dr. Bethune, would you tell her I got an *A* on my report?"

She smiled again. "Oh, splendid for you. Yes, I'll surely tell her." She got back into the car, and it rolled away.

Elmo, Delmo, Stella, and I watched until the car turned down a side street and disappeared. Then we started to scream and shout. "Man! We met President Franklin Roosevelt's wife!" Elmo shouted. "She shook this hand! I'm not gonna wash this hand for a week!"

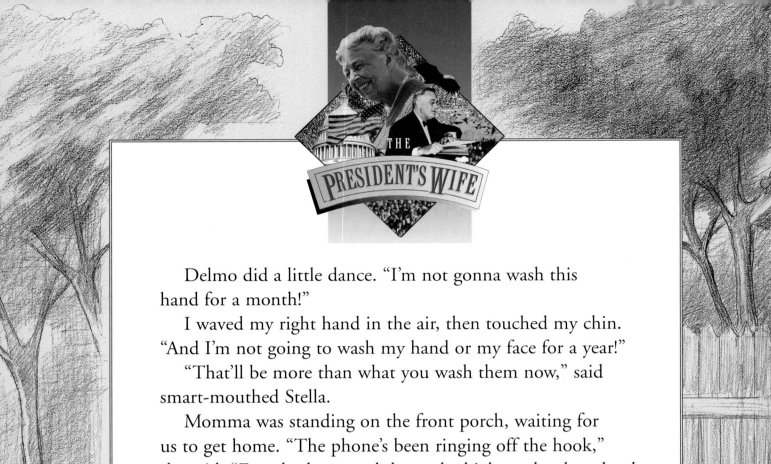

Delmo did a little dance. "I'm not gonna wash this hand for a month!"

I waved my right hand in the air, then touched my chin. "And I'm not going to wash my hand or my face for a year!"

"That'll be more than what you wash them now," said smart-mouthed Stella.

Momma was standing on the front porch, waiting for us to get home. "The phone's been ringing off the hook," she said. "Everybody up and down the highway by the school saw Mrs. Roosevelt shake your hands." She hugged Stella.

"And saw you almost get hit by her car!" She patted me all over, then hugged me.

She made us tell her everything Mrs. Roosevelt had said. Dad came out and shook our hands, too. We had to repeat everything to him.

When word got around that we had met Eleanor Roosevelt, we had to get up in school and tell the other kids what happened. We had to do it in church the next Sunday. I even had to tell it at the gas station when I went by for a pop.

I hope Mrs. Roosevelt didn't forget to give my message to Dr. Bethune. I didn't forget hers.

SOURCE
Scholastic News®
News Magazine

A 6 C D E

AWARD
WINNING

Magazine

Barbara
BUSH

First Lady of
Literacy

She calls herself "everybody's grandmother," but on January 20, 1989, Barbara Bush became America's First Lady.

The First Lady has no specific duties and does not get paid. But she is a very important person. Usually, the First Lady becomes involved in worthwhile projects. Because of her influence as the President's wife, she can make people pay attention to the issues she cares about. Rosalynn Carter, the wife of Jimmy Carter, worked to improve medical care for the mentally handicapped. Nancy Reagan is well known for her "Just Say No to Drugs" campaign.

When President Bush took office, Mrs. Bush already had her volunteer cause lined up. As First Lady, her top priority was working to eliminate illiteracy. Her interest in teaching people to read and write goes back 25 years. That is when doctors diagnosed her third son as having dyslexia (dis-LEKS-ee-ah), a reading disorder.

Mrs. Bush has campaigned for years to raise money and recruit volunteers to fight illiteracy. She even wrote a book about the family cocker spaniel, C. Fred Bush. The money from sales of the book went to literacy groups. "Some people give time, some money, some their skills and connections, some literally give their life's blood . . . but everyone has something to give," says Mrs. Bush.

"Everything I worry about would be better if more people could read, write, and comprehend," said Mrs. Bush. "I honestly don't know of a more important gift that anyone can give than the gift of literacy."

▲ Barbara Bush, **First Lady from 1989–1993 reads to a kindergarten class.**

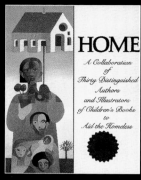

AWARD WINNING

Book

from HOME

UNDER *the* BACK PORCH

by **Virginia Hamilton**

illustrated by **Pat Cummings**

Our house is two stories high
shaped like a white box.
There is a yard stretched around it
and in back
a wooden porch.

Under the back porch is my place.
I rest there.
I go there when I have to be alone.
It is always shaded and damp.
Sunlight only slants through the slats
in long strips of light,
and the smell of the damp
is moist green,
like the moss that grows here.

My sisters and brothers
can stand on the back porch
and never know
I am here
underneath.
It is my place.
All mine.

SOURCE

CHEROKEE SUMMER

by Diane Hoyt-Goldsmith
photographs by Lawrence Migdale

Photo
Biography

From
CHEROKEE

S U M M E R

by Diane Hoyt-Goldsmith

photographs by Lawrence Migdale

My name is Bridget. I live in a small town called Okay, Oklahoma in the northeastern part of the state. In summer, the countryside is a patchwork of green pastures and golden fields. Farmers raise cotton, grain, soybeans, and corn while ranchers fatten cattle and hogs. There are dense forests of oak and hickory that shade the valleys, and rolling fields of hay that ripen in the summer heat.

Before Oklahoma became a state in 1907, the place where I live was part of Indian Territory. I am a Cherokee Indian and a member of the Cherokee Nation. My people have a long history and a great heritage. Our strong traditions have given us an identity to be proud of.

AREA OF DETAIL

CHEROKEE COUNTY →

Illinois River

Tahlequah

Okay •   *Lake Tenkiller*

Muskogee

Tulsa •

★ Oklahoma City

OKLAHOMA

Summer Fun

Summer is a special time for my family. The weather is hot and humid so we go outdoors as much as possible. One of our favorite pastimes is hunting for crawdads. My father and his twin brother used to catch them when they were little boys. Now my dad is an expert.

First we drive out to Grandfather's house and fix up some gigs—poles with a fork on the end for catching crawdads. Grandfather helps us make them out of a piece of wire and river cane. He cuts the wire from a clothes hanger and with a pliers, shapes it into a fork with two prongs. Then we tie it to the cane with a piece of string.

We go hunting at Spring Creek. It flows behind the house where my father grew up. My great-grandmother, Mary Belle Russell, raised him and she still lives there.

The best place to look for crawdads is under the rocks near the banks of the creek. If we creep along quietly, we might find one lying out in clear view. Then, a quick jab with the gig and we have caught one. Sometimes we can turn a rock over slowly and find one hiding underneath.

My father is fast and catches three or four crawdads before I can even get to the water. Then he stands back and watches my brother, sister, and me. It doesn't take us long to catch enough to fill a coffee can. I usually catch the most.

Soon it's time to cook the crawdads. We build a twig fire on the shore with some dry leaves, tiny pieces of wood, and bits of wild grapevine.

After we get the fire going, we fill the can that holds the crawdads with water from the creek. We heat the can

on stones over the fire. Soon the water starts to boil. When the crawdads turn a bright red, they are cooked and ready to eat. Nothing is more delicious than a fresh crawdad cooked over a twig fire on a hot summer day.

Bridget's grandfather splits a piece of river cane and puts the double-prong fork into the end to make a gig for catching crawdads.

Bridget's mother has gone hunting for crawdads every summer since she was a child. Breaking the sticks into small pieces, she helps her husband start a fire on the shore to cook the crawdads.

The Cherokee Language

My mother's parents can both speak our native language. Although my grandmother reads and writes in Cherokee, many of the younger people have stopped learning and using the language altogether.

Grandmother teaches the Cherokee language in an adult class during the school year. She has taught me a few words in Cherokee, and I like having a Cherokee name. Grandmother says that there are things she can say in Cherokee that are hard to translate into English. Our language is part of our history and our identity as a tribe. That is why we don't want to lose it.

The Cherokee language is spoken by combining eighty-five different sounds. The written language has a separate character for each sound, so Cherokee is written by using this syllabary, rather than by using an alphabet.

The Cherokees have had a written language since 1821. The syllabary was the invention of a man named Sequoyah. The English alphabet took four thousand years to develop, but Sequoyah invented our syllabary in just nine years.

**kah-MAH-mah
BUTTERFLY**

**yo-nah
BEAR**

**ee-NAH-dah
SNAKE**

The Cherokee Syllabary

		1 (a)	2 (e)	3 (i)	4 (o)	5 (u)	6 (v)
1		D	R	T	Ꭴ	Ꮎ	i
2	(d/t)	Ꮣ	W	ᏍᏬ	ᏗᏘ	V	S	ᏛᏯ
3	(dl/tl)	Ꮪ Ꮭ	Ꮮ	C	Ꮰ	Ꮱ	P
4	(g/k)	S Ꮩ	Ᏼ	Y	Ꭺ	J	E
5	(gw/kw)	Ꮟ	Ꮶ	Ꮲ	Ꮴ	Ꮽ	Ꮛ
6	(h)	Ꮋ	Ꮌ	Ꭿ	Ꮰ	Ꮐ	Ꮫ
7	(j/ch)	G	V	Ꮵ	K	Ꮷ	Ꮸ
8	(l)	W	Ꮁ	Ꮅ	Ꮆ	M	Ꮑ
9	(m)	Ꮿ	Ꮓ	H	Ꮹ	Ꮍ	
10	(n/hn)	Ꮎ Ꮏ	Ꮐ	Ꮒ	Ꮓ	Ꮔ	Ꮕ
11	(s)	Ꮝ Ꮎ	Ꮸ	Ꮙ	Ꮑ	Ꮏ	R
12	(w/hw)	Ꮐ	Ꮰ	Ꮙ	Ꮼ	Ꮽ	6
13	(y/hy)	Ꮿ	ß	Ꭹ	Ꮇ	Ꮍ	B

Durbin Feeling

PRONUNCIATION GUIDE

The following is a list of the roman alphabet used in Cherokee speech: a, ch, d, e, g, h, i, j, k, l, m, n, o, s, t, u, v, w, y. The consonant sounds are the same as in English. The vowel sounds used in Cherokee speech have only one sound for each:

a, as in ah	o, as in note
e, as in they	u, as in true
i, as in ski	v, as uh in huh

By combining the consonants and vowels listed by lines and columns in the chart, the correct pronunciation for each Cherokee syllable can be produced.

Example: The pronunciation for G is "ja". W is "la"; and Y is pronounced "gi" as in "buggy."

Exceptions to the rule that Cherokee syllables are produced by combining consonants and vowels are the syllables D R T Ꭴ Ꮎ i, and Ꮝ. The characters in the first line are produced by the single vowel sounds; and the character Ꮝ is simply an "s" sound.

When Sequoyah created our written language, he could neither read nor write in English. He watched the Europeans write and receive letters, and decided to come up with the same system for his own people.

Sequoyah was very artistic and the characters he drew for the Cherokee syllabary were done with a calligrapher's grace and beauty. Later on, as people began to use the syllabary to print books and newspapers, many original characters were changed to look more like English letter forms. However, in Cherokee the letters stand for different sounds. For example, a "D" in Cherokee stands for the sound "ah" and an "R" stands for "eh."

The Nation's TSA-LA-GI (*TSA-lah-gee*) Library is located in the old prison building. The people who work there try new ways of teaching children to become literate in the Cherokee language. For example, the Nation has a program in which Cherokee is taught in the schools. There is even a new computer program for students learning our language. When you type the sound of a Cherokee word on the computer, a mechanical voice pronounces it. Then the proper letter comes up on the screen. It is fun to use.

Another way to teach the language is by telling stories. The library puts on puppet shows in the schools, and the actors use Cherokee stories, characters, and words.

For our people, legends have been a good way for the elders to teach children about Cherokee life and the proper way to behave. Sometimes the stories explain something about the natural world. The stories almost always have a moral, and they are entertaining too.

Possum Learns a Lesson

A CHEROKEE LEGEND
retold by Sequoyah Guess

Long, long ago in the days when animals could talk, Possum had a big, bushy tail. It was even more beautiful than Fox's, and Possum was proud of it. He loved to show it off to his friends. Every day he combed it a hundred times to keep it looking shiny.

The rest of the animals grew tired of Possum's showing off. They got together and discussed what they could do to teach him a lesson. Then they came up with a plan.

Rabbit went over and talked to Possum.

"We're going to have a dance tonight," he said, "and it's in honor of your tail."

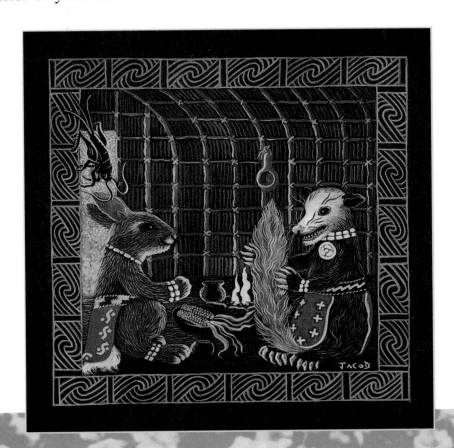

"Great! Great!" Possum replied. "But you know I'll need a special chair to sit on so I can show it off."

"Of course," Rabbit answered. "We'll get a nice chair for you. But in the meantime, I'll help you get ready. You won't have to do a thing. Just sit back and relax."

Possum was really thrilled to have so much attention paid to his tail. He lay back while Rabbit carefully washed and combed it. Possum was so relaxed and happy that he soon fell asleep.

While Possum snored peacefully, Rabbit whistled for his friend Cricket. It was time to put the rest of the plan into action. Cricket came and shaved off all the hairs on Possum's tail. Then he helped Rabbit wrap some cloth around it.

When Possum woke up, Rabbit told him, "I've got this cloth over your tail to keep it nice for tonight." Possum didn't give it a thought. He was full of excitement and couldn't wait for the dance to begin.

When night came, all the birds and the animals gathered for the dance. Chanting their ancient songs, they moved around the fire in a perfect circle, singing and dancing.

Rabbit said to Possum, "You should go out there and dance. We are all waiting to see your most wonderful tail." As he spoke, he started to unwrap Possum's tail.

Possum was in such a hurry to dance that he didn't look back. He did not notice that anything was wrong. He danced and sang, circling the fire with a huge grin on his face.

"Look at my tail," he sang. "I've got a beautiful tail. There's no tail like mine."

The animals started to giggle. They said "Oooooh!" and "Aaaaah!" Then they started to laugh out loud.

At first, Possum thought they were admiring his tail. He kept on singing. Each time he passed the animals, he sang "Look at my beautiful tail!" But the more the animals laughed, the more Possum wondered, What's wrong? Why are they making fun of me?

Then he turned and looked behind him. His beautiful tail was pink and bare! Instead of being big and bushy, it was skinny and ugly.

Possum was so embarrassed that he fell backward, his big smile frozen on his lips.

Possum never got his bushy tail back. And to this day, all opossums have a hairless tail. If you startle an opossum when you are walking in the woods, he'll play dead and grin just like Possum did. Possum learned it is not smart to brag about anything too much.

A Summer Stomp Dance

For the Cherokees, dancing around a fire is not something that only happens in legends and stories. Special stomp dances are still held every weekend all year round by the traditional people in the tribe. Our people keep the spirit of ancient teachings alive by singing the songs that we have learned from past generations. Because these have never been written down, the elders teach the words and melodies to their children. Attending a stomp dance has become a very special part of my summer.

Before the dances begin, the Cherokees often prepare a special feast called a "Hog Fry." Everything is cooked outdoors over an open fire. It takes all afternoon to make an evening meal for the crowd.

The Cherokees are known for their hospitality. It is a tradition that anyone who comes to a stomp dance will be fed. The meal is a time for sharing. It creates an atmosphere of friendship for the dances that follow.

Stomp dances have been performed for centuries. They are still danced by the tribes of the Southeast—the

Small pieces of pork are added to hot lard in a cast-iron kettle to cook. The stove was made out of a fifty-gallon oil drum. A hole for adding wood has been cut into the sides near the bottom.

Cherokees, Creeks, Seminoles, and Shawnees. The dancers believe that the rhythmic songs and movements of the dance help put them back in balance with the world. Dancing gives them peace of mind.

Men, women, and children are free to participate in the dances. Children begin to dance when they are very young, following the movements of their parents and grandparents.

At a stomp dance, dancers from many tribes gather to visit, feast, and worship. The dances begin after dinner and usually last all night long.

Some of the girls wear a modern version of shackles, made with tin cans rather than turtle shells. The cans make a nice sound when filled with tiny pebbles.

On long summer afternoons, when I have the chance to be alone, I like to draw pictures and let my mind wander. I dream about what I will do when I grow up and how I will live. Perhaps I'll be an artist or a dancer. I might be a doctor or a teacher. I might even be the chief of my tribe.

For now, I feel lucky to have a loving family and to live in a beautiful place. I am proud of my Cherokee heritage, and I will work hard to keep it strong. Soon it will be time to go back to school. The weather will turn cold and the leaves will fall. But I will have the memories of this Cherokee summer—a special time in my life.

The summer hay crop near Tahlequah is harvested and collected into bales for drying. The giant hay rolls are a good place to be alone to think and dream.

AWARD
WINNING

Book

from FAMILY PICTURES

• Cuadros de familia •

by CARMEN LOMAS GARZA

The pictures in this book are all painted from my memories of growing up in Kingsville, Texas, near the border with Mexico. From the time I was a young girl I always dreamed of becoming an artist. I practiced drawing every day; I studied art in school; and I finally did become an artist. My family has inspired and encouraged me for all these years. This is my book of family pictures.

Los cuadros de este libro los pinté de los recuerdos de mi niñez en Kingsville, Texas, cerca de la frontera con México. Desde que era pequeña, siempre soñé con ser artista. Dibujaba cada día; estudié arte en la escuela; y por fin, me hice artista. Mi familia me ha inspirado y alentado todos estos años. Este es mi libro de cuadros de familia.

Oranges

We were always going to my grandparents' house,
so whatever they were involved in we would get involved in.
In this picture my grandmother is hanging up the laundry.
We told her that the oranges needed picking so she said,
"Well, go ahead and pick some." Before she knew it, she had
too many oranges to hold in her hands, so she made a basket
out of her apron. That's my brother up in the tree, picking
oranges. The rest of us are picking up the ones that he
dropped on the ground.

Naranjas

Siempre íbamos a la casa de mis abuelos, así que cualquier
cosa que estuvieran haciendo ellos, nosotros la hacíamos
también. En este cuadro, mi abuela está colgando la ropa a
secar. Nosotros le dijimos que las naranjas estaban listas para
cosechar, y ella nos respondió:—Vayan pues, recójanlas. En un
dos por tres, tenía demasiadas naranjas para sostenerlas en las
manos, así que convirtió su delantal en canasta. Ése es mi
hermano, en el árbol, recogiendo naranjas. El resto de nosotros
estamos recogiendo las que él deja caer al suelo.

Watermelon

It's a hot summer evening. The whole family's on the front porch. My grandfather had brought us some watermelons that afternoon. We put them in the refrigerator and let them chill down. After supper we went out to the front porch. My father cut the watermelon and gave each one of us a slice.

It was fun to sit out there. The light was so bright on the porch that you couldn't see beyond the edge of the lit area. It was like being in our own little world.

Sandía

Es una noche calurosa de verano. Toda la familia está en el corredor. Mi abuelo nos había traído unas sandías esa tarde. Las pusimos en el refrigerador para enfriarlas. Después de la cena, salimos al corredor. Mi padre cortó la sandía y nos dio un pedazo a cada uno.

Era divertido estar sentados allá afuera. La luz del corredor era tan fuerte que no se podía ver más allá del área que estaba iluminada. Era como estar en nuestro propio pequeño mundo.

How to
Write a
Personal
Narrative

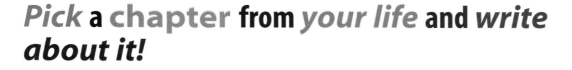

Pick a chapter from your life and write about it!

Ever think about writing a book starring you as the main character? Many authors do just that when they write a personal narrative. In a personal narrative, authors share their memories and experiences with others. Each story is told using the first-person point of view, as though the author is speaking directly to the reader.

1 Choose a Story to Tell

Decide on a topic for your personal narrative. Think of important events in your life that you'd like to share with others. If you made a Table of Contents, you may want to use one of your chapter title ideas. After you've decided what to write about, ask yourself these questions. What is my story about? When did it happen?

Where did it take place? Who else was there? Think about these questions when you're writing your outline.

Tips
- Ask your family for details about the event you chose for your story.
- What age were you when the story took place?
- What did you look like?
- Write your story as though you are talking to a friend.

TOOLS

- notebook and pencil
- memories about events in your life
- people who can help you remember dates and details

2 Make an Outline

Now that you have your story idea, it's time to organize your material. Like any story, your personal narrative should have a beginning, a middle, and an end. Think about the story you want to tell, and divide your paper into three sections. Then write a few sentences in each section that tell what happened in that part of your story. This outline will help you organize your personal narrative.

How Am I Doing?

Before you start writing, take a few minutes to ask yourself these questions.

- Do I have a clear idea of what I want to write about?

- Have I decided on the mood of my story? Is it funny, sad, or something else?

- Is the outline of my story clear and organized?

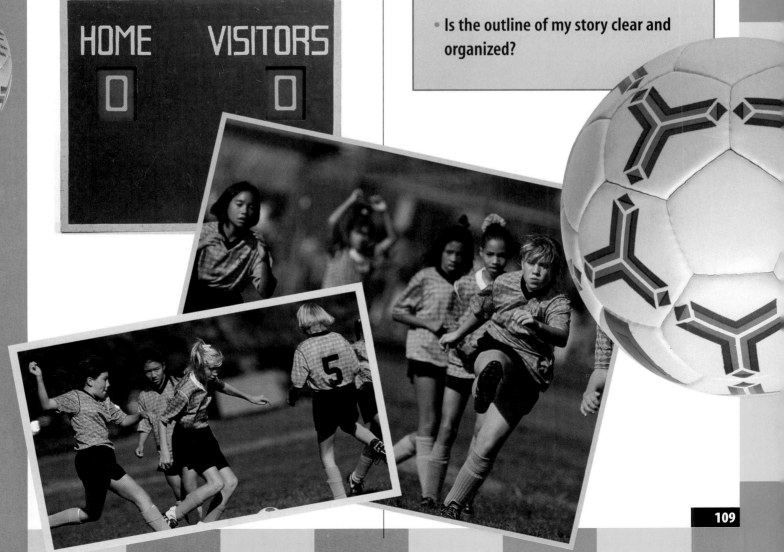

3 Write Your Personal Narrative

Once you've finished your outline, it's time to write your story. Use the ideas in your outline, and then add lots of details. Search your memory to find sensory details that will make your personal narrative come alive. What sounds, tastes, and smells do you remember? What colors remind you of the event you are writing about? Be sure to write your story using the first-person point of view.

4 Present Your Story

Here are some ways to present your story. Whatever form you choose, illustrate your narrative with drawings or photos.

- Make a book by stapling several sheets of paper together. If you made a book jacket, you can use that as the cover!

- Create a poster by arranging your writing with pictures and photos on a piece of posterboard.

- Write to a friend and tell your story in letter form.

- Turn your narrative into a script for a play.

- If you want to, you can share your personal narrative with the rest of the class.

If You Are Using a Computer . . .

Try drafting your personal narrative in the Report format on the computer. Choose clip art to illustrate your work. To make your narrative ready to present, you can print it out and use the book cover from Workshop 2, or you can make a new title page. If you like, you also can use the Record and Playback Tools as you work on your story.

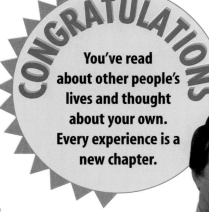

CONGRATULATIONS

You've read about other people's lives and thought about your own. Every experience is a new chapter.

Jerry Spinelli
Author ▶

Glossary

a·pol·o·get·ic
(a pol′ə jet′ik) *adjective*
Regretful. After he dropped the plate, he gave her an *apologetic* look.

ath·lete (ath′lēt) *noun*
A person who has the skills to do well in sports or physical exercise.

athlete

au·di·ence
(ô′dē əns) *noun*
The people who read an author's work. She is a successful author because she has a large *audience*.

brusque·ly
(brusk′lē) *adverb*
A rough and abrupt manner of doing something. She *brusquely* slammed the door.

bur·lap (bûr′lap) *noun*
A rough cloth woven from jute or hemp.

cal·lig·ra·pher
(kə lig′rə fər) *noun*
A person who has beautiful handwriting. He asked a *calligrapher* to write the invitations.

Word History

The word **calligrapher** comes from the Greek word *kalligraphia*. The word *kallia* means "beauty," and the word *graphein* means "to write."

ca·pa·ble
(kā′pə bəl) *adjective*
Competent. She is a *capable* driver in wet weather.

char·ac·ter
(kar′ik tər) *noun*
Any letter, symbol, or figure that is used in writing. The letter *A* is a *character* in the English alphabet.

con·so·nant
(kon′sə nənt) *noun*
Any letter of the alphabet that is not a vowel.

con·tent
(kən tent′) *adjective*
Satisfied and happy.

con·ver·sa·tion
(kän′ver sā′shən) *noun*
The act of talking with another person. She had a long *conversation* with her teacher.

ed•i•tor (ed´i tər) *noun*
A person who checks and corrects a piece of writing so that it is ready for publication.

ed•u•ca•tor
(ej´ ə kā´tər) *noun*
A person whose job it is to teach or train others.

ep•i•sode
(ep´ə sōd´) *noun*
One event in a series of events.

et•i•quette
(et´i kit) *noun*
Rules for good behavior. It is good *etiquette* to chew with your mouth closed.

fair (fâr) *adverb*
According to the rules. He didn't play *fair*.

Word Study

The word **fair** can be used to mean:
• attractive
• a clear, sunny day
• a just and honest person

---

fu•ri•ous
(fyoor´ē əs) *adjective*
Very angry.

in•flu•ence
(in´floo əns) *noun*
The power to have an effect on or change others. The teacher was a good *influence* on him.

in•volved
(in volvd´) *verb*
Engaged in. She became *involved* in many projects.
▲ **involve**

---

laughed (laft) *verb*
Made an amused sound because something was funny. ▲ **laugh**

laughed

lit•er•ate
(lit´ər it) *adjective*
Able to read and write.

a	add	ŏŏ	took		ə =
ā	ace	ōō	pool		a in *above*
â	care	u	up		e in *sicken*
ä	palm	û	burn		i in *possible*
e	end	yōō	fuse		o in *melon*
ē	equal	oi	oil		u in *circus*
i	it	ou	pout		
ī	ice	ng	ring		
o	odd	th	thin		
ō	open	ŧh	this		
ô	order	zh	vision		

Glossary

man·ners
(man′ərz) *noun*
Good behavior. It's good
manners to thank your
host after a party.

nov·els (nov′əlz) *noun*
Long fictional stories.
She read three *novels* by
the same author. ▲ **novel**

pat·tern
(pat′ərn) *noun*
The way in which shapes
and colors are placed to
form a design.

pub·lished
(pub′lisht) *verb*
Printed and offered for
sale. Her book was
published this summer.
▲ **publish**

puz·zled
(puz′əld) *verb*
Confused. His bad
behavior *puzzled* her.
▲ **puzzle**

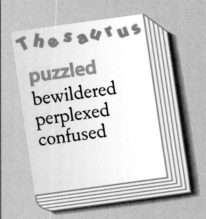

Thesaurus

puzzled
bewildered
perplexed
confused

quilt (kwilt) *noun*
A bed covering made
from pieces of fabric
stitched together.

sat·is·fied
(sat′is fīd′) *adjective*
Contented. She was
satisfied with her
finished story.

pattern

quilt

sched·ule
(skej′ o͞o əl) *noun*
A list of times at which to
do certain things. He had
an exercise *schedule* which
he followed faithfully.

scraps (skraps) *noun*
Small bits and pieces that are leftovers from something larger. ▲ **scrap**

Thesaurus

scraps
remnants
odds and ends
bits and pieces

small talk
(smôl′ tôk′) *noun*
A light conversation about everyday things.

stitched (sticht) *verb*
Sewed together. She *stitched* the quilt together from scraps. ▲ **stitch**

syl•la•bar•y
(sil′ə ber′ē) *noun*
A writing system in which each sound of a spoken language is expressed by a different character or letter.

scowled (skould) *verb*
Frowned and looked threatening. The bully *scowled* at the boy.
▲ **scowl**

syl•la•bles
(sil′ə bəlz) *noun*
Words or parts of words pronounced with a single uninterrupted sound. The word butterfly has three *syllables*. ▲ **syllable**

trans•late
(trans′ lāt) *verb*
To put into the words of a different language. She was able to *translate* French into English.

vol•un•teer
(vol′ən tēr′) *adjective*
Doing a job without pay. She was a *volunteer* firefighter.

vow•el (vou′əl) *noun*
One of the sounds represented by the letters *a,e,i,o,u,* or sometimes *y.*

wool•en
(wŏŏl′ən) *adjective*
Made of wool.

a	add	ŏŏ	took	ə =	
ā	ace	ōō	pool	a in *above*	
â	care	u	up	e in *sicken*	
ä	palm	û	burn	i in *possible*	
e	end	yōō	fuse	o in *melon*	
ē	equal	oi	oil	u in *circus*	
i	it	ou	pout		
ī	ice	ng	ring		
o	odd	th	thin		
ō	open	th	this		
ô	order	zh	vision		

Authors & Illustrators

Pam Conrad *pages 10–21*

When Pam Conrad was seven, she got chickenpox. Her mother gave her some paper and colored pencils. Instead of drawing, she began to write poetry. She kept on writing, and in the fourth grade she won a writing contest. The prize was a puppy! Now Pam Conrad writes books that are inspired by her childhood memories and things that happened to her children. Her daughter Sarah was the inspiration for *Staying Nine*.

Virginia Hamilton *pages 84–85*

Virginia Hamilton comes from a long line of storytellers. Her parents told stories so often that soon it became natural for her to do the same. The author of many award-winning books, Ms. Hamilton still lives in her hometown of Yellow Springs, Ohio.

Diane Hoyt-Goldsmith
Lawrence Migdale *pages 86–99*

A beautiful piece of Native American art inspired Diane Hoyt-Goldsmith to research her first book, *Totem Pole*. She teamed up with photographer Lawrence Migdale for the project, and they have continued to work together on many other books.

Lauren Mills *pages 40–53*

Lauren Mills learned quilting, weaving, and doll making from her mother, grandmother, and aunt. The songs and stories of the Appalachian people inspired her to write *The Rag Coat*. They reminded her of the patchwork coat she once wore.

Gary Soto *pages 54–61*

Many of Gary Soto's stories and poems have been inspired by his Mexican-American heritage and his childhood in Fresno, California. Mr. Soto didn't begin writing until he was in college, where he discovered his love of poetry. Today, Gary Soto is known for his essays and stories, as well as his poetry. In his stories, humor always plays an important part.

Eleanora E. Tate *pages 70–81*

Eleanora Tate's happy childhood inspired her to write stories for children. She gets her ideas from the people around her; then she makes her stories larger than life so that others will want to read them.

"Childhood can be happy if children learn that they can do anything they set their minds to, if they try."

Books &

Author Study

More by Jerry Spinelli

Dump Days
In this funny book, two friends find adventure in an unusual place.

Picklemania!
Pickles, Salem, Eddie, and Sunny make sure that life at Plumstead School is never dull!

Report to the Principal's Office
Pickles the skateboarder and his three friends are all trying to adjust to a new school, but each of them goes about it in a different hilarious way.

Fiction

Mieko and the Fifth Treasure
by Eleanor Coerr
Mieko dreamed of becoming a great artist, but that was before her hand was injured. Now she can barely hold a paintbrush. Will she ever be able to paint again?

Sara Crewe
by Frances Hodgson Burnett
In this classic book, Sara's world is turned upside down when her father dies. Once she was treated like a princess at Miss Minichin's Select Seminary for Young Ladies. Now that she is poor, she lives in the attic and wears ragged clothes.

Nonfiction

Bicycle Rider
by Mary Scioscia
illustrated by Ed Young
When bicycle racing first gained popularity as a sport, Marshall Taylor was one of the fastest racers in the world. This book tells how he became the first African-American professional racer.

Silent Observer
by Christy MacKinnon
Over a hundred years ago, this author was born on a farm in Canada. Through her own words and original watercolor paintings, MacKinnon describes the fun she had with her seven brothers and sisters, as well as her experiences when she left home to study at the Halifax School for the Deaf.

&Media

Videos

Anne of Green Gables
Disney Home Video
In this classic story, Anne finds a new family and a new life on Prince Edward Island in Canada. (202 minutes)

The Pool Party
Reading Adventures
Gary Soto's novel is brought to life in this humorous film. (30 minutes)

Marshall Taylor

Software

Bank Street Writer
Broderbund Software (Macintosh, Apple, MS-DOS)
Here's a program to help you write your life story—or anything else you would like to write. In the network version, you can share the stories and messages you create with others.

Charlotte's Web
(A Write On! Multimedia Story)
Humanities Software (Macintosh, Apple II, MS DOS)
This version of E. B. White's classic book includes a video and computer activities.

Magazines

Stone Soup: The Magazine by Children
Children's Art Foundation
This magazine wants your writing and artwork. It publishes stories, poems, and pictures done by kids.

Storyworks
Scholastic Inc.
Storyworks has great art, fiction, real-life stories, and interviews. And in every issue kids tell about the books they like and why they like them.

A Place to Write

**The Giraffe Project,
197 Second Street
Langley, WA 98260**

Here's an organization that celebrates acts of courage and kindness. Write to find out how you or someone you know can qualify for future awards.

Acknowledgments

Grateful acknowledgment is made to the following sources for permission to reprint from previously published material. The publisher has made diligent efforts to trace the ownership of all copyrighted material in this volume and believes that all necessary permissions have been secured. If any errors or omissions have inadvertently been made, proper corrections will gladly be made in future editions.

Cover: Illustration from FAMILY PICTURES by Carmen Lomas Garza. Copyright © 1990 by Carmen Lomas Garza. Reprinted by permission of Children's Book Press. Border by Vicki Wehrman.

Interior: "Class-Picture-Taking Day" and cover from STAYING NINE by Pam Conrad. Text copyright © 1988 by Pam Conrad. Cover illustration copyright © 1988 by Mike Wimmer. Reprinted by permission of HarperCollins Publishers.

Excerpts from BIG SCIENCE: BONES AND MUSCLES. Copyright © 1990 by Scholastic Inc. Reprinted by permission.

Excerpt from the Table of Contents of BOY by Roald Dahl. Copyright © 1984 by Roald Dahl. Reprinted by permission of Farrar, Straus & Giroux, Inc. By permission also of Murray Pollinger, London.

"The Rag Coat" from THE RAG COAT by Lauren Mills. Copyright © 1991 by Lauren A. Mills. Reprinted by permission of Little, Brown and Company.

Excerpt and cover from THE POOL PARTY by Gary Soto. Text copyright © 1993 by Gary Soto. Cover illustration copyright © 1993 by Robert Casilla. Used by permission of Delacorte Press, a division of Bantam Doubleday Dell Publishing Group, Inc.

Excerpts and cover from PENNY POLLARD'S GUIDE TO MODERN MANNERS by Robin Klein, illustrated by Ann James. Text copyright © 1989 by Robin Klein. Illustrations copyright © 1989 by Ann James. Published by Oxford University Press. OXFORD is a trademark of Oxford University Press. Used by permission.

Cover from WHEN I WAS NINE by James Stevenson. Copyright © 1986 by James Stevenson. By permission of Greenwillow Books, a division of William Morrow & Company, Inc.

"The President's Wife" and cover from FRONT PORCH STORIES AT THE ONE-ROOM SCHOOL by Eleanora E. Tate. Text copyright © 1992 by Eleanora E. Tate. Used by permission of Bantam Books, a division of Bantam Doubleday Dell Publishing Group, Inc. Cover illustration by Eric Velasquez. Used by permission of the illustrator.

"Barbara Bush" from *Scholastic News*, April 14, 1989. Copyright © 1989 by Scholastic Inc. Reprinted by permission.

"Under the Back Porch" by Virginia Hamilton, illustrated by Pat Cummings. Text copyright © 1992 by Virginia Hamilton, illustration copyright © 1992 by Pat Cummings. All selections from HOME edited by Michael J. Rosen. Copyright © 1992 by HarperCollins Publishers. Jacket illustration by Leo and Diane Dillon. Jacket illustration copyright © 1992 by Leo and Diane Dillon. Reprinted by permission.

"Cherokee Summer" adapted from CHEROKEE SUMMER by Diane Hoyt-Goldsmith, with photographs by Lawrence Migdale. Text copyright © 1993 by Diane Hoyt-Goldsmith. Photographs copyright © 1993 by Lawrence Migdale. Text illustrations copyright © 1993 by Murv Jacob. Maps copyright © by Square Moon Productions. The new version of the Cherokee syllabary is used courtesy of Durbin Feeling of the Tsa-La-Gi Library, Tahlequah, OK 74465. Reprinted by permission of Holiday House.

Excerpts and cover from FAMILY PICTURES by Carmen Lomas Garza. Copyright © 1990 by Carmen Lomas Garza. Reprinted by permission of Children's Book Press.

Cover from FOURTH GRADE RATS by Jerry Spinelli, illustrated by Paul Casale. Illustration copyright © 1991 by Paul Casale. Published by Scholastic Inc.

Cover from THE LAST PRINCESS: THE STORY OF PRINCESS KA'IULANI OF HAWAI'I by Fay Stanley, illustrated by Diane Stanley. Illustration copyright © 1991 by Diane Stanley Vennema. Published by Simon & Schuster Books for Young Readers, Simon & Schuster Children's Publishing Division.

Cover from MY NAME IS MARÍA ISABEL by Alma Flor Ada, illustrated by K. Dyble Thompson. Illustration copyright © 1993 by K. Dyble Thompson. Published by Atheneum Books for Young Readers, Simon & Schuster Children's Publishing Division.

Cover from STEALING HOME by Mary Stolz, illustrated by Pat Cummings. Illustration copyright © 1992 by Pat Cummings. Published by HarperCollins Children's Books, a division of HarperCollins Publishers.

Photography and Illustration Credits

Photos: © John Lei for Scholastic Inc., all Tool Box items unless otherwise noted. p. 2 tl, bl: © John Bessler for Scholastic Inc. pp. 2-3 background: © John Lei for Scholastic Inc. p. 3 bc: © John Lei for Scholastic Inc.; tc: © Ana Esperanza Nance for Scholastic Inc. p. 4 tc: © Ana Esperanza Nance for Scholastic Inc.; cl: Susi Dugaw for Scholastic Inc.; c: © Ana Esperanza Nance for Scholastic Inc.; baby: © The Stock Market; bc: © Ken Karp for Scholastic Inc.; cr: © Scott Harvey for Scholastic Inc.; tr: © Focus on Sports p. 5: © Ana Esperanza Nance for Scholastic Inc. p. 6: © Ana Esperanza Nance for Scholastic Inc. pp. 8-9 © Buckley School Collection/Superstock. pp. 12, 16, 18, 21: © Susi Dugaw for Scholastic Inc. pp. 22-23 cl: © Don Mason/The Stock Market; all others: © Ken Karp for Scholastic Inc. p. 24 bl: © M. Elaine Adams/Little Brown. p. 25 cr: courtesy of Jerry Spinelli. p. 26: © Focus on Sports. p. 27 tr: © Ken Karp for Scholastic Inc.; br: courtesy of Jerry Spinelli; bl: © Richard Megna/Fundamental Photographs for Scholastic Inc. p. 28 tr: © I. Bernard/Animals Animals; cl: © Zig Leszcynski/Animals Animals; br: © Comstock. p. 29 cl: courtesy of Jerry Spinelli. p. 30 cl: © Scott Harvey for Scholastic Inc.; tr: © John Bessler for Scholastic Inc.; tl, bl: © John Lei for Scholastic Inc.; c: © Ana Esperanza Nance for Scholastic Inc. p. 31 c: © Scott Harvey for Scholastic Inc.; cr: © John Bessler for Scholastic Inc. p. 32 bl: © John Bessler for Scholastic Inc.; br: © Scott Harvey for Scholastic Inc. p. 33 cr: © Scott Harvey for Scholastic Inc.; bl: © John Bessler for Scholastic Inc. p. 36 bl: © Richard Kaylin/Tony Stone Images, Inc.; tr: © Robert P. Carr/Bruce Coleman Inc.; br: © Rainer Grosskopf/Tony Stone Images Inc. p. 37 bl: © Stanley Bach for Scholastic Inc.; tr: © Spencer Jones/FPG International Corp.; br: © Scott Harvey for Scholastic Inc. pp. 38-39 Private Collection/Superstock. pp. 64-65 border: © Paul Halagan; c: © John Lei for Scholastic Inc. p. 66 br: © Stanley Bach for Scholastic Inc; cl: © Bob Torrez/Tony Stone Images, Inc. p. 67 br: © Scott Harvey for Scholastic Inc. pp. 68-69 © Private Collection/A.K.G., Berlin/Superstock. p. 82 cl: © Cynthia Johnson/The Gamma Liaison. p. 83 br: © Brad Markel/The Gamma Liaison. pp. 86-87 © Lawrence Migdale. p. 89 tr: © Lawrence Migdale; bl: © Tony Stone Images. p. 96 bl: © Lawrence Migdale. pp. 97-99: © Lawrence Migdale. pp. 106-107: © John Lei for Scholastic Inc. p. 107 tr: © Craig Tuttle/The Stock Market. p. 108 bl, cr: © John Lei for Scholastic Inc.; br: © Stanley Bach for Scholastic Inc.; cl: © David Young-Wolf/Photo Edit. p. 109 cl, br: © John Lei for Scholastic Inc.; bc: © David Madison; tr: © Stanley Bach for Scholastic Inc. p. 110 c: © Stanley Bach for Scholastic Inc.; bl: © John Lei for Scholastic Inc.; tr: © Don Mason/The Stock Market tr, bl: (leaves): © Don Mason/The Stock Market. pp. 110-111 c: © Stanley Bach for Scholastic Inc. p. 111 bc: © Don Mason/The Stock Market; tr: © Don Mason/The Stock Market; br: © Scott Harvey for Scholastic Inc. p. 112 bl: Comstock, Inc. p. 113 cr: © Jeff Isaac Greenberg/ Photo Researchers, Inc. p. 114 cl: © Bill Longcore/ Photo Researchers, Inc. pp. 114-115 tc: © "The Greenhouse Effect" by Sally A. Sellers. p. 116 Virginia Hamilton: © Carlo Ontal; Diane Hoyt-Goldsmith: © Holiday House; Pam Conrad: © Sarah Conrad. p. 117 Eleanora Tate: © Zack E. Hamlett, III; Gary Soto: © courtesy of Scholastic Trade Department; Lauren Mills: © Little Brown & Company. p. 119 bl: © Schomburg Center for Research in Black Culture; br: © Stephen Ogilvy for Scholastic Inc.

Illustrations: pp. 11-21: Joel Spector; pp. 40, 42, 44-47, 49-50, 53: Hugh Harrison; pp. 54-61: Tony De Luz; pp. 70-81: Eric Velasquez; p. 86-99 border: © Lawrence Migdale; p. 101: Jessica Wolk-Stanley, spot art.